'I AM MYSELF A

‡

NELSON, THE NORFOLK HERO

FURTHER DETAILS
OF POPPYLAND TITLES
CAN BE FOUND AT
www.poppyland.co.uk
WHERE CLICKING ON THE
'SUPPORT AND RESOURCES' BUTTON
WILL LEAD TO PAGES
SPECIALLY COMPILED TO

'I am myself
a Norfolk Man'

NELSON, THE NORFOLK HERO

BY

Charles Lewis

POPPYLAND
PUBLISHING

First published 2005
ISBN 0 946148 72 4

Published by Poppyland Publishing, Cromer NR27 9AN

Picture credits

Lindsay Blackmore: p. 139
Eastern Daily Press: pp. 135 (left), 143 (top)
Great Yarmouth Borough Council and Norfolk Nelson Museum: p. 89
Charles Lewis: pp. 131 (top), 134 (top)
The National Archives: pp. 30–31
Norwich Castle Museum and Art Gallery: pp. 2, 85
Paston College collection: pp. 11, 22, 25, 105, 131 (middle), 132
Christopher Pipe/Watermark: p. 15
Poppyland Photos: pp. 10, 17, 20, 21, 24, 32, 33, 37, 40, 41, 44, 45, 48, 53, 54, 57, 59, 73, 77, 84, 93, 100, 107, 123, 127, 130, 131 (right), 138 (top), 143 (bottom)
R. C. Fiske collection: pp. 8, 12, 14, 18, 23, 27, 28, 29, 34, 36, 47, 61, 64, 65, 67, 68, 71, 75, 79, 81, 86, 92, 96, 97, 102, 103, 112, 113, 114, 115, 118, 119, 120, 124, 128, 129, 132, 134 (middle), 137, 138 (bottom)
Norfolk Nelson Museum: p. 135 (right)

Designed and typeset in 11 on 17pt Minion by Watermark, Cromer NR27 9HL

Printed by Printing Services (Norwich) Ltd

Frontispiece: Portrait of Nelson by Sir William Beechey, commissioned by the City of Norwich. Nelson sat for it in London early in 1801. Probably the most heroic of his portraits, it shows to Nelson's right the Spanish admiral's sword which he had presented to the city of Norwich, and to his left, probably, the cocked hat which he wore at the Nile and which he gave to Beechey. The sword and hat are now in the Castle Museum, Norwich, and the portrait hangs in the Blackfriars Hall.

For Juyna and Anna

Acknowledgements

This book is written in memory of many happy hours spent talking Nelson with Ron Fiske and the late Ben Burgess while working on Ben's collection. Ben was always happy to accommodate anyone with an interest in Nelson and his enthusiasm infected many, including myself.

I am particularly indebted to Ron Fiske, who has been very generous with his time and expertise in reading and commenting on the manuscript, correcting errors and making invaluable suggestions.

Contents

Viscount Nelson, Baron of the Nile and of Burnham Thorpe
with emblems of his life and naval victories by J. J. Hall of Great Yarmouth

A Norfolk Man

BY 1800 NELSON, now 41, a rear-admiral and a peer, and
the victor of one of the greatest naval battles ever fought (at the
Nile in August 1798), might be expected to have left his roots
far behind. On his return to England that year, however, he
declared to an adoring crowd at Great Yarmouth, 'I am myself
a Norfolk man and I glory in being so'.[1]

It was not just a cheap crowd pleaser. There is ample evidence to show that Norfolk always held a special place in his
affections. Indeed, he kept at least a hint of a Norfolk accent
and a Norfolk manner of speech. In 1801 a midshipman on the
Monarch, then in the Baltic, remembers Nelson being rowed
across to his ship. He recalled that 'a squeaking little voice
hailed the Monarch and desired us, in true Norfolk drawl, to
prepare to weigh'.[2]

Nelson was born in Burnham Thorpe in the north-west of
the county. His family was a large one and had friends and relations spread across the county. He went to school in Norwich
and North Walsham before joining the navy at the age of 12.
His career brought him briefly back to the shores of Norfolk
during the next few years although most of this period was
spent in American and Caribbean waters.

The ending of the War of American Independence saw him
without a ship or post and so he returned to Burnham Thorpe,

The village sign in Burnham Thorpe, unveiled in 1975.
The sign was presented by the Royal Navy, having been made in
the workshops of HMS Sultan, the Navy's engineering school at Gosport.

with his new wife, to spend five rather fretful years. Once war

broke out with revolutionary France in 1793 he was recalled to sea and seven years elapsed before he again set foot in Norfolk. This was on his triumphal return from the Mediterranean and was the occasion of his address at Yarmouth.

His last visit to Norfolk was during the following year, 1801, when he joined the fleet at Yarmouth preparing for the Copenhagen campaign, returning there after the victory.

Whilst he was at sea Norfolk was not forgotten, for Nelson was a prolific letter writer and his family and Norfolk friends were always to be found among his correspondents. He provided financial help to his family when he could and used what influence he had on their behalf when asked. At Christmas there were often gifts for the poor of Burnham Thorpe.

Whenever thoughts of life after the navy came to mind he imagined retirement in Norfolk. When he was ennobled in 1798 he chose a title reflecting his pride in his origins – Baron Nelson of the Nile and of Burnham Thorpe.

Writing to Dean Allott from the Victory *in 1804, Nelson remembers his birthplace with nostalgia.*

In his will Nelson entrusted his precious daughter Horatia to Lady Hamilton but after her death Horatia went to live with Nelson's sister, Catherine Matcham, and her family and then with the family of his brother-in-law Thomas Bolton in Burnham Market, just a few miles from Nelson's birthplace. She spent 17 years there before, by a happy twist of fate, she married the local curate, Philip Ward.

Many other Norfolk men served in the navy during Nelson's time, not a few of whom were attracted to the service by the example of Nelson himself. This admiration was reciprocated, for Nelson is reported to have favoured Norfolk seamen as recruits, saying he 'always reckoned them as good as two others'.[3]

Nelson's victories were celebrated with pride in his home county. Norwich presented him with the Freedom of the City and both Yarmouth and Thetford presented him with Freedoms of the Borough. After his death the people of Norfolk subscribed to the erection of a monument in his memory which was built at Yarmouth some thirty years before the more famous one in Trafalgar Square.

His memory is still celebrated across the country in that most English of styles, in pub names. The *Nelson Arms*, *Nelson's Head* and the *Lord Nelson* are all to be found, but the one of which he might have been most proud is the *Norfolk Hero*.

Engraving by S. Read after J. Greenaway (Illustrated London News, 3rd June 1882), showing Yarmouth harbour entrance and South Denes looking much as in Nelson's time but with the Nelson Monument in the centre of the picture.

A Norfolk Family

NELSON DID NOT come from a background of wealth nor of poverty but from the unpretentious comfort of the country church. Both his father and paternal grandfather were clergymen but some additional social standing came from his mother's side where there were connections to the aristocracy.

His family was a large and close one and his parents had an important influence on him. His father, Edmund, was a modest man, an upright and loving parent who once wrote:

> as to the society in me I never mixed with the world enough at a proper period in life to make it entertaining or valuable on any account except a willingness to make my family comfortable when near me and not unmindful of me when at a distance.[4]

It seems evident that this is indeed how his family felt. Edmund also had a poetic bent which revealed itself in his letters to his children. Here he is writing to his youngest daughter Catherine on 1st January 1787:

> December has visited us with all the pomp and parade of Winter, wind and storm and rattling Hail; cloathed with frosted robes, powdered with snow, all trimmed in Glittering Icicles; no blooming Dowager was ever finer.

Edmund came from a clerical background. His father, also Edmund, was Rector of East Bradenham, and vicar of Sporle (from about 1725) until he became Rector at Hilborough in 1734 on the presentation of his father-in-law, John Bland. He died there in 1747 aged 54. Edmund was born at East Bradenham on 19th March 1723, the second son in a family of eight (two of whom died in infancy). After school at Scarning, Northwold and Swaffham he went on to Caius College, Cambridge in 1742. He became curate for his father at Sporle in 1745 and then curate at Beccles in Suffolk in 1747. There he met Catherine Suckling, living nearby with her widowed mother. When his father died later that year Edmund succeeded him to his livings at Hilborough (on his mother Mary's presentation – she had received the advowson as a gift from her father) and Sporle (from the Provost and fellows of Eton). He determined to live on the proceeds of Sporle, giving up his Hilborough income to pay off his father's debts and support his mother and family who remained there with him. In May 1749, however, he married Catherine Suckling at Beccles and they moved to a house in Swaffham, where their first three children were born. In 1753 they moved to a rented house at Sporle.

Catherine Nelson appears to have been a more lively and outgoing character than her husband. Her eldest daughter remembered that she was 'quite a heroine for the sailors'[5] and Nelson himself remembered that 'she hated the French'.[6] She also had family connections on a higher social scale than her husband's. Her father, the Rev. Dr Maurice Suckling, had been Rector of Barsham in Suffolk and Prebendary of Westminster

Nelson's father, Rev. Edmund Nelson, rector of Burnham Thorpe from 1755 until his death in 1802. (Engraving by W. C. Edwards, 1845.)

but his father and grandfather had both been High Sheriffs of Norfolk. Her mother, Anne, was the daughter of the influential Sir Charles Turner of Warham. Anne's mother, Mary, was sister of Horatio, first Baron Walpole of Wolterton and of Sir Robert Walpole of Houghton, first Earl of Orford (and famous in history as Britain's first Prime Minister). Through the Walpoles there were links to yet another of the great landed families of Norfolk, for one of her grandmother's sisters had married Lord Townshend of Raynham.

The Nelson family was proud of these connections and although there was never any social relationship with the Townshends, or indeed the Walpoles at Houghton, the family did became regular visitors at Wolterton.

Wolterton Hall

The Nelsons had a large family, Catherine giving birth to 11 children altogether. The boys, however, seemed to have been rather fragile, for three of them died in infancy. Their first son, Edmund, was born in 1750 but lived only four months. He was buried at Hilborough. Horatio, born the following year, was not quite four months old when he died and was buried at Hilborough. He had been named after the first Baron Walpole who had stood as one of his sponsors. Maurice, born in 1753, was the first of their children to survive, followed in 1755 by Susannah (Sukey), born at Sporle.

That same year Edmund became Rector of Burnham Thorpe, Burnham Norton, Burnham Ulph and Burnham Sutton (the latter two now part of Burnham Market), sponsored by Horatio Walpole, later the first Baron Walpole of Wolterton. The rectory at Burnham Thorpe now became the family home and seven more children were to be born there: William in 1757, Horatio in 1758, Ann (Nanny or Nancy) in 1760, Edmund (Mun) in 1762, Suckling in 1764, George in 1765 (who died at six months old and is buried in the church) and finally Catherine (Kate or Kitty) in 1767.

A Norfolk Childhood

THE RECTORY AT Burnham Thorpe was a modest L-shaped red brick building comprising a two-storey wing attached to another which was single storeyed but with an attic floor lit by dormers. It stood in 30 acres (12 hectares) of glebe land with barns and stables and with a hillside behind from which the sea was visible. It was here that Horatio Nelson was born on 29th September 1758, coincidentally in the same year that William Pitt ordered the building of the *Victory*.

Whilst most authorities agree, and indeed Nelson himself stated, that he was born in the rectory, alternative sites have been suggested, possibly satisfying a need for the hero to have made a more dramatic appearance. They range from a local barn to a heap of stones by the roadside. One account suggests that Nelson was born in a nearby house owned by Lord Orford, the family having apparently moved there while the rectory was under repair following a fire.[7] A house named the Shooting Box is associated with the same or a similar story. [8] Another story suggests that his birthplace was Ivy Farm (near to the public house) where his mother was taken when she went into labour whilst out in a coach.[9]

The rectory stood close to the present road leading to the village. A plaque on the roadside wall of the rectory grounds records the spot. After the death of Nelson's father in 1802 the new rector, Daniel Everard, had the old rectory pulled down in 1803 and built a new one further up the hill. This building still survives but was replaced as rectory by a house built close

The site of Nelson's birthplace today. The plaque records that the old parsonage stood 20 yards back from the wall. Part of the old building may survive in the section with the television aerial.

*Burnham Thorpe
rectory (engraving
after J. Pocock). Nelson
was born here in 1758.
It was pulled down in
1803.*

to the church in 1956. On the site of the old rectory he built a coach house, stables, and quarters for his coachmen and grooms. An oil painting of the old rectory survives and well illustrates the power of the Nelson legend. After Nelson's death there was considerable public demand for mementoes of the hero and a host of prints, paintings and other souvenirs were commissioned. One thing missing, however, was a picture of Nelson's birthplace. The fact that it had been pulled down did not hinder the artist Pocock who apparently got the Nelsons' nearest neighbour and distant cousin Henry Crowe to draw a sketch from memory, and this Pocock turned into a painting.

Nelson was privately baptised on 9th October and was then publicly christened at the parish church on 15th November. The second Horatio, Baron Walpole of Wolterton, acted as godfather. Although christened Horatio he was known in the

family as Horace and there is an entry in the parish register for
1769 where, having acted as a witness to a village wedding, his
signature, Horace, has been corrected by his father to Horatio.

Life at Burnham seems to have been idyllic and Nelson
had, to all appearances, a normal and happy early childhood.
From the birth of Catherine in 1767 the household comprised
the rector and his wife, eight children and the family servants
who included 'Will, indoors', 'Peter, without', and 'Nurse Blackett'. Nurse Blackett eventually left the rectory and married Mr
High, landlord of the Old Ship Inn at Brancaster.[10]

As playmates Nelson had his family, particularly William
who was nearest to him in age, and there were frequent trips
to his cousins at Hilborough. His aunt, Alice Bland, married
Robert Rolfe (a fellow of Caius, and so perhaps introduced by
Edmund, who married them by licence) in 1760 and when Edmund moved to Burnham, Rolfe was presented by his mother-
in-law to the Rectory at Hilborough. Nelson's Rolfe cousins
were Edmund and Robert (both destined for the church, and
Robert to become domestic chaplain to Nelson), Randyll and
Ellen. Other relations included uncle Maurice who had a house
at Woodton, south of Norwich.

Other family friends included the Crowes at Burnham
Thorpe Hall, Sir Mordaunt Martin at Burnham Westgate with
his seven daughters and one son, and Canon Charles Poyntz of
North Creake (Kitty's godfather).

A few anecdotes survive from Nelson's childhood. Chosen
clearly to show the embryonic hero and no doubt improved
by early authors they do apparently originate from the family.
One story tells that on a visit to his grandmother at Hilborough on one occasion, he and a friend went bird nesting. His

grandmother got worried when they had not returned by dinner time and sent people to search for them. They were found at last sheltering under a hedge and counting over their spoils. Scolding him on his return his grandmother said 'I wonder fear did not drive you home' to which Nelson's reply was 'Madam, I never saw fear'.[11]

Another late bird nesting expedition on the hill behind the rectory was cut short by Nurse Blackett who sent him to bed. Later that night, however, he got up and returned to the wood where he was found fast asleep in the morning.

Another night time excursion was undertaken in response to a dare and involved a midnight trip in winter to the churchyard bringing back as proof a branch of yew.

His sense of honour is illustrated by the occasion on which he and his brother William set off for school one snowy winter morning. They decided that the bad conditions were excuse enough to miss school and returned home. Their father, however, asked them to try again, saying 'I leave it to your honour not to turn back unless necessary'. Trying again, William was eventually all for returning but Horatio insisted on going on, saying 'Remember, brother, it was left to our honour'.[12]

It is likely that Nelson's earliest education was at Bunting's school in the village, of which his father was a trustee, though there is no evidence for this.

In 1767 Nelson and his brother William were sent away to the Norwich School in the Cathedral Close, Norwich. A number of relatives lived in the

The Carnary chapel in the cathedral close, Norwich. This was part of the Grammar School in Nelson's day and is still the school chapel.

city, including a cousin, Mrs Berney, a paternal aunt, Mrs Thomasine Goulty, and a great aunt, Mrs Sarah Henley (both the latter living in St Andrew's parish) and it is possible that the boys boarded with one of these, perhaps the Goulty family.

William and Horatio's stay at the Norwich school was short lived, for in December that year their mother died and the family's world was turned upside down. Catherine Nelson was just 42 when she died. Her daughter Susannah was of the opinion that 'she had bred herself to death.' The rector was left with eight children to look after. Catherine, the youngest, was just nine months old and was probably unaffected by her mother's death but Horatio was nine and the evidence suggests that he was deeply affected. Thirty-seven years later, in May 1804, he was at sea in the Mediterranean and reminded of Burnham by a letter from Richard Allott, Dean of Raphoe in Ireland. (Allott's brother had been rector at Burnham Norton and an acquaintance of Nelson.) He replied, 'Pardon this digression: but the thought of former days brings all my Mother into my heart, which shows itself in my eyes'.[13]

For the rector there were practical matters to consider and

Stone in Burnham Thorpe church commemorating Nelson's mother Catherine, daughter of Dr Maurice Suckling and wife of Rev Edmund Nelson his brothers-in-law were able to help. Maurice, at 15, was the oldest child at home. His uncle William Suckling, a Commissioner in the Customs Office and living in Kentish Town, now found him a position as a clerk in the Excise Office.

Probably on Maurice Suckling's recommendation, the next two boys, William and Horatio, were moved in 1768 to the Paston School at North Walsham. It was then gaining itself a good reputation with a new headmaster, John Price 'Classic' Jones, and new buildings. In 1802 Levett Hanson, a former schoolfellow, wrote to Nelson: 'I well remember where you sat in the schoolroom. Your station was against the wall, between the parlour door and the chimney . . . Nor do I forget that we were under the lash of Classic Jones, as arrant a Welshman as Rees-ap-Griffith, and as keen a flogger as merciless Busby, of birch-loving memory'[14]. Another teacher at the school, an elderly Frenchman, was known as 'Jemmy Moisson'. Another childhood tale attests to Nelson's character, for he was dared one night to steal pears from 'Classic' Jones's garden. He successfully brought them back to his dormitory and when a reward of five guineas was offered the next day for information about the thief, no one betrayed him.[15]

*'Nelson's brick' at
Paston College*

There is a recollection of Nelson catching measles at school and being nursed by a Miss Gaze[16] and he also seems to have indulged in other typical schoolboy activities. One of the school's treasures is a brick, now broken in two halves, carved with the initials H. N. It was discovered in the east wall of the playground in 1881. William Haggard, an old boy of the school, was visiting the school with his son, the writer Henry Rider Haggard, and

remembered the brick which had been known as 'Nelson's brick'. A search by lantern light located it and it was promptly removed to the schoolhouse.[17]

Some biographers have suggested that Nelson went to school in Downham Market. The origins of this are a number of ambiguous statements by Capt. Manby. George William Manby has some fame as the inventor of the line-throwing mortar apparatus for rescuing shipwrecked sailors, which he first demonstrated in 1807 at Great Yarmouth. He was born near Denver in Norfolk in 1765 and went to Downham Market school in 1770. He published various accounts of his life in which he appeared to suggest that Nelson was at school with him there. Nelson, however, was seven years older than Manby and in 1770 was most certainly at school in North Walsham.

Captain G. W. Manby, shown with a picture illustrating one of his inventions for rescuing people from shipwreck which he developed whilst Barrack Master at Great Yarmouth. (Pencil drawing by C. J. W. Winter, Great Yarmouth.)

One unpublished manuscript autobiography by Manby offers a version which hints at the reality of any relationship. He writes that he was sent to school at Downham in 1770 and 'at the same time Horatio, afterwards Lord Nelson, was with Mr Noaks with whom I was most intimate'.[18] Whilst this might suggest that Noaks may have been a teacher at North Walsham, there is no record of him there. It is interesting to see that despite the fact that Nelson was not at Downham Market, there are nevertheless anecdotes recalling his time there! One recalls Nelson floating paper ships in the water pumped by his school friends from the pump in the main street. Another records him visiting a shoemaker who worked for the school and accidentally breaking a pet lamb's leg by crushing it in the shop door.[19]

The best authority for Nelson's schooldays must be his brother William, who stated in 1834 that he had no recollection of Nelson going to school in Downham Market, adding:

Plaque on Paston College's 18th-century building, recording Nelson's schooldays there.

We both went to school at Norwich some time in the year 1767 and remained there about two years. We were then removed to North Walsham. My brother was with me till the spring of the year 1771, when he went to sea, leaving me there till I went to Cambridge in the year 1774.[20]

Nelson's education at the Paston School clearly served him well. Colin White, Nelson author and scholar, believes that the history and literature he learned there, under 'Clas-

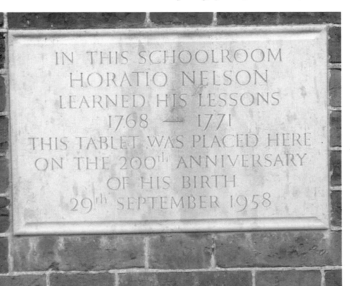

IN THIS SCHOOLROOM
HORATIO NELSON
LEARNED HIS LESSONS
1768 — 1771
THIS TABLET WAS PLACED HERE
ON THE 200th ANNIVERSARY
OF HIS BIRTH
29th SEPTEMBER 1958

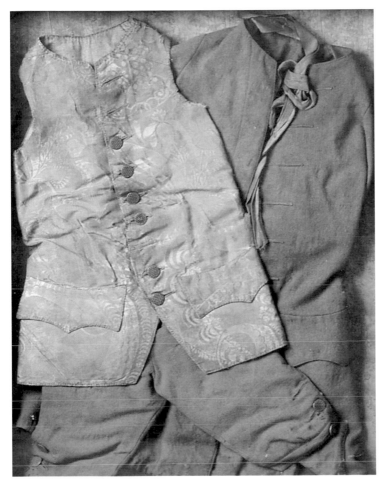

This suit of clothes, comprising jacket, waistcoat and breeches, is part of the Paston College collection and is reputed to have been worn by Nelson. There is no conclusive evidence to support this claim, but the clothes are certainly typical of his time.

sic' Jones, taught him about leadership. Indeed, he probably learnt by heart there the famous St Crispin's Day speech from Shakespeare's Henry V, from which he borrowed to describe his captains after the Nile as his 'band of brothers'.

It was during the Christmas holiday of 1770–71 that Nelson read some momentous news in the local newspapers. Britain had been at peace since the end of the Seven Years War in 1763 but now there was the threat of war again. A dispute with Spain about sovereignty over the Falklands had become serious after the Spanish had landed there and lowered the British flag. A task force was being assembled to sail to the area and unemployed naval officers were finding themselves recalled to duty. Among these was Nelson's uncle, Maurice Suckling, who had been appointed to the command of the *Raisonable* (64 guns), a French ship captured in the year of Nelson's birth.

Maurice was a naval captain but had not had a command since the end of the Seven Years War. In June 1764 he had consolidated his links with the Walpoles by marrying Mary Walpole, daughter of the first Baron, and they had been living quietly at Woodton Hall. Maurice was, however, something of a hero in the family. In October 1757, a year before Horatio was born, he had been engaged in a stirring action in the Caribbean. Then in command of the *Dreadnought* (60), and in company with two other ships, another 60 and a 64, he engaged seven French ships off Cape Francois. They comprised four ships of the line, including two 74s and a 64, and three frigates. After two and a half hours the French withdrew, one of their frigates taking the flagship under tow.[21] The anniversary of this battle used to be celebrated annually in the Nelson household. It had taken place, ironically, on 21st October (later, of course, the date of Trafalgar).

There had, in fact, been a naval tradition of sorts in the Walpole family. Richard Walpole, brother to Nelson's godfather, had served on East Indiamen and in 1755 had been in action, with other East India Company ships, against two French warships, which had been repulsed.[22] Of more significance was Captain Galfridus Walpole who died in 1726. Galfridus had fought in the War of English Succession, and, like Maurice, had been involved in one particularly noteworthy action. In the Mediterranean in March 1709, as captain of the *Lion* (60) he had been engaged by four French ships of 60 guns each. In an uncanny parallel to Nelson he lost his right arm to a cannon ball during the action. The sword that he had been carrying passed in due course to Maurice who in turn left it to Nelson and Nelson was carrying it himself when he lost his right arm at Tenerife in 1797.[23]

News of uncle Maurice's appointment excited Nelson. A naval career, he saw, was an opportunity not only for adventure and glory, but also a way of relieving his father of some of his family responsibilities and achieving something which would make his father proud. He got his brother William to write to his father, then at Bath, for his permission to go to sea. With, no doubt, a mixture of misgivings and relief his father passed on the request and in due course there came an accommodating, though not entirely encouraging, reply from Maurice:

What has poor Horace done, who is so weak, that he above all the rest should be sent to rough it out at sea? But let him come; and the first time we go into action, a cannon-ball may knock off his head, and provide for him at once.

There had clearly been an expectation that Maurice would help out at some stage in providing for one of the boys, but that it should turn out to be Horace was quite a surprise.

Nevertheless, Nelson was duly rated as midshipman on the books of *Raisonable* from January 1771. He was just 12 years and three months old; not, in fact an uncommon age at which to start a naval career. Although he had now been entered on the ship's books (so his seniority could be reckoned from that date) his uncle had no use for him straight away and he

Captain Maurice Suckling, RN, Nelson's uncle. He rose to become Comptroller of the Navy and was instrumental in encouraging Nelson's early career. (Engraving by Ridley, 1805.)

returned to school for the Spring term. It was not until March that he finally left for sea. Peter 'without', the family servant, came to school to collect him and take him to King's Lynn. There he joined his father on the coach to London. Together they stayed overnight at uncle William's house in Kentish Town until the following morning when Nelson embarked alone on the Chatham coach to join the *Raisonable* there. It was for Nelson to make his own way in the world now, assisted by whatever interest his uncle could exercise on his behalf.

A Seagoing Apprenticeship

Nelson embarking on his first voyage (Illustrated London News, 20th October 1906). Nelson is depicted on the steps at Chatham, about to embark for his uncle's ship, Raisonable, in 1771.

MAURICE DID INDEED do what he could to ensure that Nelson progressed. As it happened, the Falklands affair blew over, *Raisonable* was paid off, and Maurice was transferred to the *Triumph* (74), on guard duties in the Thames. He could see that this would provide scant opportunities for his nephew and arranged for Nelson to get some seagoing experience on a merchant ship destined for the West Indies. To maintain continuity of service, Maurice rated him as Captain's servant until his return, when he became Midshipman on *Triumph* again. His West Indian voyage had an unexpected result. He wrote later: 'I returned a practical Seaman with a horror of the Royal Navy . . . It was many weeks before I got in the least reconciled to a Man-of-War, so deep was the prejudice rooted.'[24]

Sensing this, no doubt, his uncle encouraged his urge for experience and it was probably he who provided Nelson with an introduction to Captain Skeffington Lutwidge of the *Carcass* in 1773. *Carcass* and *Racehorse*, two little bomb ketches, were being fitted out for an expedition to the Arctic to search for a north-east passage and Nelson's enthusiasm had been fired by the prospect. As a result of the introduction he was able to secure a place aboard as coxswain of the Captain's gig. The expedition certainly provided excitement and is noteworthy for another revealing anecdote. The earliest version, for a sketch of Nelson published in the *Naval Chronicle* in 1800, recalled that Nelson was discovered missing one night while the ship was icebound. In the early light he was spotted some distance from the ship carrying a musket and pursuing a polar bear. The musket wouldn't fire but Nelson was apparently hoping to tire the bear before dispatching it with the butt. When he returned to the ship Nelson's explanation of his conduct to the captain was: 'I wished, Sir, to get the skin for my father'.[25] Later versions of the story were much more elaborate, to make even more evident the ambition, courage and filial respect of the hero to be. A contemporary account from a log written aboard suggests only that a bear, which got too close to the ship, ran

Nelson's encounter with the polar bear, 1773 (from Orme's Graphic History of the Life, Exploits, and Death of Horatio Nelson, 1806). This is probably the first depiction of this incident.

Week Days	94° D.	Winds	Courses	dist.	Lat. de	Long. de made	Bearings and distances at Noon.
September 1773							
Thursday 16.	11	SWbW WbW West NWbW	S11°W	70	By Obs.n 53°.34′	12°.8′W	Hackluit's Headland N11°.30′E dist. 157/8 miles.
Friday 17.	11	West NW WbNW	S23°E	22	53°.14′	12°.54′W	Cromer light House SWbW 4 or 5 leagues.
Saturday 18.	11						Anchored in Yarmouth Roads. Yarmouth Church N15°W Gullstone Church NWbW about 2 miles

Return to Norfolk: extract from the log of the Carcass mentioning Cromer lighthouse, which is also seen in the extract from a chart prepared in the 1790s. At this date the light was still a coal fire.

away when approached by some of the crew members. *Carcass*'s passage to and from the Arctic would have taken her past the Norfolk coast. It provided Nelson with, probably, his first view of his native land from the sea. On 18th September 1773,

Remarks onboard His Majesty's Sloop *Carcass*. 1773.

First part Fresh Gales and squally, middle Fresh Breezes with rain, latter Fresh Breezes and Cloudy, at 2 PM wore to the NW, set Fore topsail and out reefs, at 5 moderate, out reefs, at 7 in 1st. and 2d. reefs, at 8 AM several fishing vessels in sight, at 9 got a Pilot from one of them, and wore to the Nd ward, at 10 TKd to the SW, sounded every hour.

First part Fresh Gales and Cloudy, middle Strong Gales, latter Moderate and Cloudy, at 4 PM TKd to the NW, at 7 in 3d. reefs, at 8 in Fore and Mizon topsls at 10 in Maintopsail, ½ past 11 wore to the Sd ward, soundings 5 fathoms, at 4 AM wore to the Nd ward, carried away several lanyards of the lower rigging, at 6 set Topsails, and out 3d. reefs, at 8 up Topgallt. yards and out 2d. reefs, at 10 made the Land from NW b W to W S. find the Ship above two degrees to the Eastward of the Reckoning.

Fresh Breezes and Clear, at 10 PM anchored with the Best Bower in 12 fath. Winterton Ness lights S b W about 4 miles, ½ past 4 AM Weighed and came to sail, and at 9 AM Anchored in Yarmouth roads in 7 fathoms, at Noon sent away an Express to the Admiralty with a Journal of the Proceedings of the Voyage.

during the return voyage, the ship put into Yarmouth and remained there for a few days.

Maurice's name helped Nelson arrange his next posting, as Midshipman on the frigate *Seahorse* (20), bound for the East Indies. He was away for two and a half years, during which he succumbed to a serious bout of fever (possibly malaria). On his return he found that his uncle's star had risen, for Maurice had been appointed Comptroller of the navy, one of the most influential posts in the service. Once again Maurice helped him get a posting, this time as an acting lieutenant, on the *Worcester* (64), sailing on convoys between England and Gibraltar. By April 1777 Nelson had had enough years of service to present himself, with his journals, for examination as Lieutenant. When he first entered the Admiralty room to face the examining board, 'he at first appeared somewhat alarmed'.[26] It was not surprising, for his uncle was in the chair. Maurice, however, gave no sign of recognition and it was not until Nelson's promotion had been unanimously agreed that he introduced his nephew to the other officers present. When asked why he had not informed them earlier, the Comptroller replied: 'I did not wish the younker to be favoured. I felt convinced he would pass a good examination, and you see, gentlemen, I have not been disappointed.'[27] Back at uncle William's in Kentish Town Nelson was able to celebrate with sisters Nancy and Sukey who were visiting, and with his father who arrived a few days later.

*Burnham Thorpe
church tower*

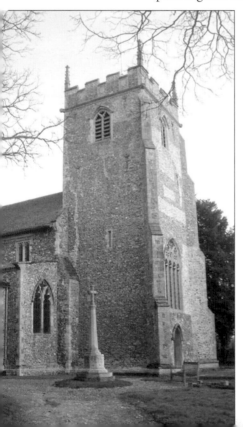

Nelson was now appointed Second Lieutenant of the frigate *Lowestoffe* (32 guns), the last occasion on which his uncle may have had any influence on his career, for Maurice died suddenly in July 1778. From Maurice's estate there were inheritances of £500 each for Nelson and his brothers, and of £1,000 each for his sisters. The remainder was left to Maurice's brother William, including Galfridus Walpole's sword which he was to pass to Nelson, for shortly before his death Maurice had confided to the Rector that he would live to see his son an Admiral. Nelson acknowledged the debt he owed his uncle in a letter to his other uncle, William:

I trust I shall prove myself, by my actions, worthy of supplying that place in the service of my country which my dear uncle left me.[28]

Service now kept Nelson away from Norfolk for the next three years, much of it spent in the Caribbean where he contracted a tropical disease (or perhaps a recurrence of the one he had caught in the East Indies) and was invalided back to England. After a period of convalescence at Bath, and with uncle William in Kentish Town (which became his base whenever he was in the capital) he was able to make a brief visit to Burnham, with his brother Maurice, in the summer of 1781. Maurice was now Clerk of the Foreign Accounts in the Navy Office, a move engineered, no doubt, by his uncle Maurice shortly before his death.

Burnham was now a much quieter place. Only Catherine, aged 14, was still at home. Susannah had left home at the age of 18 as apprentice for three years to a milliner in Bath and had then become a shop assistant there. After receiving two legacies, one from Mr Norris of Witton, a family friend, and then one from uncle Maurice, she gave up her job and returned to Norfolk. In August 1780 she was married by her father, at Burnham, to Thomas Bolton, a coal and corn merchant of Wells. They were now living at

Wells harbour. Wells claims its links with Nelson as an important harbour in his youth, a place of dispatch for his goods, his links with the Wells Club and a continuing link through Horatia (see p. 126).

Wells and Susannah was pregnant, giving birth in November to twin girls, Elizabeth and Emily. Both Thomas and Nelson's brother William seem to have been members of the Wells Club, which met for cards twice a week in the Three Tuns or the Royal Standard in the town, and it is likely that Nelson was taken there on occasion during his visit. Writing to William later (September 1781) Nelson asked that 'you must not forget me to your Wells' Club, nor anywhere else where I am known'.[29] Writing again in October he sent 'Compliments to the Wells' Club, and all friends in Norfolk'.[30]

William himself was now a clergyman, having graduated from Christ's College, Cambridge, and been ordained in June 1781.

This 1797 engraving by Shipster is taken from the first known portrait of Nelson, painted by J. F. Rigaud between 1777 and 1781.

The Young Captain

NELSON WAS ONLY to spend a few weeks at home, for in August 1781 he was appointed Captain of the frigate *Albemarle* (28) and by the 23rd of the month he was at Chatham to inspect her. He seemed keen to recruit Norfolk men with whom he would feel comfortable and he wrote to brother William:

> *If you will ask Forster to enter for the Ship, he shall be rated master's-mate, and receive five pounds bounty money; and if he can bring any Seamen with him, shall have two pounds for each man, and they will have the same bounty. They can come by any of the Wells ships, who will be paid for bringing them.*[31]

Some arrived whom he was pleased to get. One was 'John Oliver, belonging to Wells, and [I] have made him a Quartermaster; he is a very good man'.[32] Nelson also had to deal with all of those trying to obtain posts for themselves or others on the strength of their acquaintanceship. In a letter to William in October he wrote: 'The Collector's letter I have received, and have sent for the young man'.[33] The Collector was probably Charles Boyles, Collector of Customs at Wells. Even brother Edmund seems to have been seeking an appointment on behalf of someone, for in the same letter Nelson wrote: 'I received a letter from Mun and am much obliged to him for the trouble he has been at. All I can say in answer to it is that Mr Wiseman is a goose.' Two weeks later he wrote: 'tell him (Mun) I would not take either Mr Wiseman or Walker. I hardly think I have such a bad man aboard'.[34]

Brother William had decided that a seagoing life might suit his ambitions and Nelson now had to look into this for him. He wrote:

> *I have talked with Mr Suckling* [uncle William] *about your going Chaplain in the navy, and he thinks, as I do, that fifty pounds where you are, is much more than equal to what you can get at Sea; but in that I know you will please yourself, therefore shall not attempt to state any argument to dissuade you from it.*[35]

William, however, was persistent and Nelson replied to another of his letters in September:

> *I have not seen one creature, since I have been in Town, that I can talk to upon the subject; but be assured I shall not forget you . . . As to my real opinion, whether or no you will like it, I say, as I always did, that it is five to one you will not.*[36]

Again in October he was writing: 'Your matter, as yet, I have made little progress in'.[37]

Nelson was in Yarmouth Roads for nearly two weeks in December 1781. *Albemarle* had been employed to accompany a convoy of merchant ships from Elsinore in the Baltic to Portsmouth and Plymouth, and was held up by the weather at Yarmouth. The voyage from Denmark had been enlivened by one incident on 13th December, for a suspicious cutter was sighted. He wrote: 'One privateer was in our Fleet, but it was not possible to lay hold of him. I chased him an hour, and came up fast with him, but was obliged to return to the fleet. I find since it was the noted Fall the pirate'.[38]

Fall, commanding the *Sans Peur* (or *Fearnought*) out of Dunkirk, had achieved some notoriety during the previous two years along the east coast. A gravestone in St Nicholas' churchyard at Great Yarmouth (between the church and

The Albemarle *firing a gun to warn the convoy to close. Nelson was on convoy duty in the North Sea aboard* Albemarle *in 1781. The convoy was attacked by the privateer Captain Fall.*

Northgate Street) recalls one of his victims, David Bartleman,
master of the brig *Alexander and Margaret* of Shields, who died
of the wounds he suffered in an engagement with Fall in January 1781. His vessel was one of at least four taken by Fall off
Norfolk and Suffolk that month. Soon after his encounter with
Nelson, however, Fall seems to have moved out of the North
Sea and is next sighted off the west coast.

William was still keen on going to sea and Nelson tried to
dissuade him, writing from Yarmouth Roads in mid December: 'I hope you have lost all ideas of going to Sea, for the more
I see of Chaplains of Men-of-War, the more I dread seeing my
brother in such a disagreeable station of life.'[39] Nevertheless,
William came over to Yarmouth to spend a day on board his
brother's ship at the end of the month.

There were regular exchanges of letters with family while
Nelson was in home waters, sometimes involving him in deli-
cate matters. Thomas Bolton, for example
seems to have requested a loan, and Nelson found himself debating with William
the pros and cons of agreeing. In the end
Nelson suggested that 'perhaps our deny-
ing the money to Mr Bolton, may bring on
a disagreement between him and his wife
(Susannah); it is better for us to run the
risk of the sum, than to have such a thing
happen'.[40] He wrote to Bolton accordingly:
'My brother and myself have (according to
our sister's and your desire) this day wrote
to Messrs Marsh and Creed, desiring them
to pay the money to your order'.[41] William

*This gravestone, in
St Nicholas' church-
yard in Yarmouth,
commemorates David
Bartleman, master of
a Tyneside brig, who
died after an action
against the 'notorious
English Pirate Fall'
off Yarmouth on 31st
January 1781. Later
that year Fall attacked
a convoy being
escorted by Nelson.*

even seems to have visited Nelson on board at Deal in January 1782, perhaps in pursuit of his Chaplain's post.

In February Nelson was awaiting new orders and felt it politic not to forget influential relations. The Wolterton Walpoles had passed on their best wishes via William and Nelson replied: 'If I should touch on any wine Countries, you can assure Lord Walpole I will purchase some of the best wines for him.'[42] His destination, however, was not to be a wine country but North America. He sailed for Quebec in April 1782. Moving on to the Caribbean at the end of the year, he was back in England in June 1783. Paid off and with time on his hands he stayed initially in London and kept up with home news by letter. 'Nothing, I assure you can give me so much pleasure as hearing from my brothers and sisters'.[43]

At last, in late August, he set off with brother Maurice in the Lynn Diligence for a visit home.

In October 1783, Nelson decided on a visit to France and, in November, left with an old friend, Capt. Macnamara, for St Omer. There was soon a long letter to William detailing all his impressions, mostly unfavourable comparisons: 'the manners, houses, and eating, so very different to what we have in England'.[44] News from William included that of his presentation as Rector at Little Brandon. Nelson was pleased for him, and for his father: '[I] am exceedingly happy to hear of your preferment, as it will make you an independent man, and also give ease to our good Father . . . Is Little Brandon a pleasant village? Have you a good Parsonage house?'[45] The financial affairs of Thomas Bolton were still a concern: 'What is to become of Mr. Bolton? Where does he mean to fix?' Unfortunately there was also sad news, which nearly took Nelson home. Uncle William

had written to tell him of the death of his sister Anne. Anne
had been apprenticed to a lace warehouse in London but,
like Susannah, had left after receiving her uncle's legacy. She
had apparently been seduced in London and had had an il-
legitimate son, though he had been provided for by his father,
presumably in London. Now, according to Nelson, 'She died at
Bath after a nine days illness . . . it was occasioned by coming
out of the ball-room immediately after dancing.'[46] For Nelson,
'My surprise and grief upon the occasion are . . . more to be felt
than described' but, characteristically, he was worried about
the effect on his father and youngest sister:

> *I have not heard from our Father since our melancholy loss.*
> *My fears from that account are great . . . What is to become*
> *of poor Kate? . . . If such an event was to take place* [his fa-
> ther's death] *I shall immediately come to England, and most*
> *probably fix in some place that might be most for poor Kitty's*
> *advantage. My small income shall always be at her service,*
> *and she shall never want a protector and a sincere friend*
> *while I exist.*

He knew, though, what he didn't want for her: 'Although I am
very fond of Mrs Bolton [Susannah], yet I own I should not
like to see my little Kate fixed in a Wells society.'[47]

There were other things also on Nelson's mind, for he
had fallen for a young English girl staying in the same French
lodgings, a Miss Elizabeth Andrews. He wrote to brother William: 'She has such accomplishments, that had I a million of
money, I am sure I would at this moment make her an offer of
them'.[48] By January 1784 he was writing to his uncle, William
Suckling:

*Now I must come to the point; will you if I should marry,
allow me yearly £100 until my income is increased to that
sum . . . If you will not give me the above sum, will you ex-
ert yourself with either Lord North [Prime Minister] or Mr
Jenkins [Secretary at War] to get me a guard ship, or some
employment where . . . attendance . . . is not necessary.*[49]

By the time his uncle had consented, Nelson was back in England and the affair was not mentioned again. He seems to have
flirted with the idea of getting into Parliament but was soon
disillusioned. His Walpole connections were clearly of little
value to him, nor probably to his brother William who was
hoping that they would secure him a living. He wrote from
Bath in late January to William:

*Built in 1996, the
Grand Turk (here
seen at Yarmouth) is a
replica warship based
on the plans of a frig-
ate of Nelson's period.
She has been used in
films and television
programmes such
as* Hornblower *and*
Longitude.

*as to enlisting under the banner of the Walpoles, you might
as well have enlisted under those of my grandmother. They
are altogether the merest set of
ciphers that ever existed – in
Public affairs, I mean.*[50]

In the same letter, however, he
was able to report that their
father was 'never so well since
I can remember; he is grown
so lusty'.

He was thinking of spend-
ing the winter in Burnham,
where 'we shall be quite a
party', but in March 1784 he
was appointed to a new ship,
the frigate *Boreas* (28).

The Caribbean

THIS APPOINTMENT REAWAKENED his brother's interest in going to sea, and Nelson tried another tack to dissuade him, writing:

> *As to the point of carrying you in my Ship, nothing could give me greater pleasure than to have it in my power to gratify any reasonable inclination of yours, but at the present moment I do not see how you can possibly remove from Burnham.*[51]

Nelson was thinking, once again, of his father and Catherine. Someone was needed to keep them company over winter in 'that lonely place'. But William was not to be deterred and Nelson wrote from Portsmouth in April: 'Come when you please, I shall be ready to receive you. Bring your canonicals and sermons. Do not bring any Burnham servants.'[52] He didn't want his father left without help.

Boreas sailed for the West Indies in mid May and William managed to survive until late September when he finally succumbed to illness and had to be sent home. Nelson wrote to him from Antigua in late October:

> *By this time I hope you are quite recovered, and drawing near to old England. The weather has been so hot since you left us, that I firmly believe you would hardly have weathered the fever which has carried off several of the Boreas's Ship's company since you left us.*[53]

In February next year he was gently teasing William: 'I take for granted you are so much of a Sailor that you would like to hear of all our proceedings,' but reassured him, 'You may be assured I will keep you upon the Books as long as I can'. He expected that William would be back with the Wells Club: 'The Wells Club must be strong this Winter. Noisy, I'll answer, with you and him [Charles Boyles]'.[54] Boyles, son of the Collector of Customs at Wells, had been a comrade of Nelson's aboard *Raisonable*, which they had joined at the same time. Nelson often asked after him.

In December Nelson wrote to William: 'You are still on the books as Chaplain. You will accumulate a fortune if you proceed this way.'[55] He knew, though, that William was unlikely to rejoin *Boreas*. In May 1785 he had been presented to the living at Hilborough on the death of his uncle Robert Rolfe. A year later, in December 1786, Nelson wrote: 'you were discharged on 4th October.'[56] More importantly, in the same letter, he was able to congratulate William: 'So then you are at last become a husband; may every blessing attend you.' William had married Sarah Yonge at Swaffham in November 1786. Daughter of a

Devon vicar, she was sister of Chancellor Yonge of Swaffham and cousin of Philip Yonge, Bishop of Norwich.

Marriage was definitely in the air, for Nelson had news that uncle William had made an honest woman of his mistress by marrying Miss Rumsey of Hampstead in October. The following year, his little sister Catherine also wed. She had met George Matcham in Bath and the couple were married there by her father in February 1787. It was a good match, for he was as lively a character as she. He had inherited an East India fortune to which he had added before returning to England overland, later publishing an account of his travels.

As it happened, Nelson was also 'seeing' someone. In December 1786 he wrote to brother William; 'I am in a fair way to changing my situation. The dear object you must like.'[57] The 'dear object' was a young widow, Frances (Fanny) Nisbet, whom he had met in May 1785. Fanny was a few months older than Nelson. Her father, William Woolward, had been the Senior Judge of Nevis; her husband, Dr Josiah Nisbet, had been the doctor who attended him before he died. The Nisbets had moved to England but Josiah had died there in 1781. Fanny had returned to Nevis with her son Josiah, born in 1780, to live with her uncle John Herbert, the President of Nevis.

By November 1785 Nelson was writing in familiar vein to uncle William: 'My future happiness is in your power . . . if you will either give me . . . one hundred a year, for a few years, or a thousand pounds, how happy you will make a couple who will pray for you for ever.'[58] His reply and assent, written in January 1786, was received by Nelson on 8th March and a year later, on 12th March, the couple were married, on the island of Nevis.

Back at Burnham

IN JUNE 1787 Nelson was recalled home and Fanny followed on a West Indiaman. *Boreas* was paid off at Portsmouth at the end of November and Nelson was finally able to be reunited with his wife in London, where they stayed at her uncle's house.

Before they had left the Caribbean Nelson had asked his brother William to find a suitable school for Fanny's seven-year-old son, Josiah. In January 1788 he was sent to William at Hilborough (in the care of Frank Lepee, Nelson's personal servant from *Boreas*) prior to being sent on to the chosen school (presumably in Norfolk). Nelson and Fanny themselves did not get to Norfolk until the summer. An earlier visit had been considered but Fanny was not coping well with the unfamiliar cold weather, and Nelson's father, for whom socialising had never been easy, was alarmed by the prospect of meeting his new daughter-in-law. Fanny politely wrote to him from London but this only worried him more; how could rural Norfolk match what she was used to in the West Indies?

> *My very polite Correspondent . . . seems to think that it will not be many weeks before she visits these Arcadian Scenes: Rivers represented by a Puddle, Mountains by Anthills, Woods by Bramble bushes . . . Forbid it Fate.*[59]

He wrote again to daughter Catherine in March about the prospect of a visit from Captain Nelson, as he referred to him:

> *When they come into Norfolk I shall like as well if every visit is made before mine begins, and to say truth I am not now anxious to see them. Him for a day or two I should be glad of, but to introduce a stranger to an infirm and whimsical old man, who can neither eat nor drink, nor talk, nor see, is as well let alone.*[60]

In May he felt constrained to write to Nelson, writing to Catherine: 'I have requested him to not to think of bringing his Lady and Suite to Burnham till his other visits are at an end. Indeed I am in no haste to see and receive a stranger.'[61]

Nelson tactfully introduced Fanny to his family gradually. They travelled to Norfolk in the summer of 1788 but did not go straight to Burnham. Instead they went first to the Boltons, who were now at Thorpe, near Norwich. Thomas had opened an office in Ostend in September 1781 and the family had moved there in February 1782 but had returned to Wells a year later. A third daughter, Ann, was born there in August 1783 but died the following spring. They had moved to Thorpe in January 1784 and there were now four children at home including

This bust of Nelson, in Burnham Thorpe church, dates from the centenary commemoration in 1905.

Jemima and Catherine, Thomas (born in 1786) and George (born in 1787).

Living with them also was Nelson's brother Edmund. After school he had spent a seven-year apprenticeship with a Mr Havers at Wells and then had gone with brother-in-law Thomas Bolton to Ostend to work as an assistant in his office there. Returning to Norfolk later, he took a share in a ship with Bolton in 1784. Now, unfortunately, he was ill with consumption and being looked after by the Boltons.

From the Boltons, Nelson and Fanny went to the William Nelsons at Hilborough. There, brother William now had a daughter, Charlotte, born in September 1787, and his wife was pregnant again. A son, Horatio, was born in October 1788. Fanny was left at Hilborough when Nelson finally went to visit his father at Burnham, probably in the June of 1788. There he learned news of his other brothers. Suckling had gone as apprentice to Mr Blowers, a linen draper in Beccles, but had then used uncle Maurice's legacy to buy the house and business of Daines, a grocer and draper at Witton.[62] He may have moved the business to North Elmham, where he would appear to have been living in 1787 and where Nelson House on the Holt Road is recalled as the site of his shop.[63] Unfortunately the business failed and he was now at home and unsure of what to do with himself; 'there is not one ray of light which will guide us to the way he is . . . likely to walk in'[64] wrote his father to Catherine. By the summer of 1789, however, his father had persuaded him to consider a career in the church and he went to study Latin with a private tutor near Melton Mowbray.

Suckling was not the only drain on the family finances. In London, brother Maurice was now a clerk in the Navy Office, a post which had been secured for him in 1780 by uncle Maurice when he was Comptroller of the Navy. He had, however, slipped into debt and Nelson was the one to whom the Rector now looked for help. He wrote to Kitty:

> *Maurice' affairs we talked over and Hor: has undertaken and determined to go to Town in the course of a week or two and discharge all his debts and establish his future Income in a way to keep him from the necessity of being thus distressed.*[65]

Soon the Rector was able to report how Nelson had 'entirely liberated poor Maurice from the Galling chain he has long been Hampered with'.[66]

Nelson and Fanny went next to the Matchams (sister Catherine and her husband George). The couple had spent their first summer at Burnham but had taken the lease of Barton Hall on Barton Broad in the Spring of 1787. It has sometimes been suggested that Nelson learned to sail on Barton Broad and it is probably the association of his sister with Barton Hall which accounts for this. There is nothing, however, to link him with Barton before this visit except, perhaps, the memory of an elderly inhabitant who recalled the 'Nelson Oak', upon which the initials 'HN' were carved, which stood on the roadside between Barton Home Farm and Berry Hall. There is nothing,

Barton Hall, from the auction catalogue of the estate in 1935. Here Nelson visited his sister, Catherine Matcham, and her family who lived here from 1787 to 1791.

though, to suggest that Nelson ever learned to sail before joining the navy.

At last, with the Matchams as support, Nelson's father was finally introduced to Fanny and he clearly found her much less alarming than he had feared. The couple were invited to stay with him so, abandoning plans for a visit to France, they moved into the Rectory in late summer or early autumn 1788.

Nelson was to find himself living there for considerably longer than he expected. The country was at peace, so fewer ships were in commission, and Nelson's West Indian service had been the cause of some controversy, which did not make him the Admiralty's first choice for any vacant post. It was not until January 1793, when war with revolutionary France threatened, that he was finally given a new ship.

One of the first things he had to do was to make the arrangements for receipt of his half-pay, and this involved a visit to the local magistrate, Thomas Coke of Holkham Hall. Coke saw him in his study, a minor matter of routine at the time, *Holkham Hall* but now commemorated by the proud display of the chair

in which Nelson sat. In October Coke invited Nelson, Fanny and the Rector, with many others, to a festival at Holkham in November in celebration of the centenary of the 'Glorious Revolution' (the landing of William of Orange in 1688); but for reasons which might have been political or a matter of etiquette, Nelson replied that 'it is not in his Power to accept their invitation'.[67]

In 1787 George Matcham, 'Capability M' as his father-in-law described him, had persuaded the Rector that the Rectory grounds should be improved. The stream should be diverted, a pond dug and parterres, a ha-ha and other features constructed. Even after his move to Barton, the Rectory servants, with some help from the Rector and with supervisory visits by himself, carried on the work. The Rector was able to report the stream diverted in August. This was work which Nelson enjoyed, as his father told Kitty: 'your Brother is often amused in the garden, which Mr M. has engaged to beautify with some Barton roses . . . These matters are new and your bro' is happy in the thought of a future crop.'[68] Indeed, he would 'often spend the greater part of the day, and dig, as it were, for the purpose of being wearied'.[69] If only Fanny was as easily amused: 'I wish his Good Wife had her amusement; a little society and an instrument with which she could pass away an hour'.[70] However, 'She does not openly complain. Her attention to me demands my esteem, and to her Good Husband she is all he can expect.'[71]

The winter of 1788–89 was a particularly cold one and proved difficult for Nelson and Fanny who had been used to the tropical Caribbean. To Kitty the rector wrote: 'They are moving just out of the bedchamber, but both are brought to acknowledge they never felt so cold a place.'[72] Later, 'Horace has been unwell for some days, but is recovering apace. Mrs N. takes large doses of the Bed; and finds herself only comfortable when enclosed in Moreen.'[73] Life at Burnham gradually settled into a domestic pattern at the rectory with Nelson, Fanny, the Rector, the family servants, and Josiah during the school holidays. There was more work on the rectory grounds and on the rector's 30 acres of glebe. To his friend William Locker (who had been Captain of the *Lowestoffe*, on which Nelson had been first commissioned) he wrote in September 1789: 'I am now commencing farmer, though not a very large one, you will conceive, but enough for amusement.'[74] The glebe was an important source of income for his father. He continued: 'Shoot I cannot, therefore I have not taken out a licence.' There was, however, a regular family shooting party during the partridge season and Nelson is recorded as having

> *once shot a partridge; but the manner in which he carried his gun always cocked, as if he were going to board an enemy; and his custom of firing immediately when any birds appeared, rendered any attendance on him a service of considerable danger.*[75]

For Nelson, 'An Enemye floating Game is a better Mark'[76] was his father's opinion. His brother William was no more of a shot; 'the rector's fire chiefly evaporates in threats!' The best shot in the party was Thomas Bolton for 'most Bloodshed lays at T.B's door'. Coursing was, perhaps, more to Nelson's taste but even that eventually palled. In February 1792 he wrote to brother William:

> *It was not my intention to go to the Coursing meeting, for to say the truth, I have seldom ever escaped a wet jacket and a*

violent cold; besides, to me, even the ride to the Smee is longer
than any pleasure I find in the sport will compensate for.[77]

There were more gentle pastimes. He liked to go walking and
bird-nesting with Fanny. Also, apparently, he had a model
man-o'-war which he sailed on the Rectory pond. It has been
suggested that the pond, which he helped to dig, was dug in
the shape, and to the size, of a man-o'-war (possibly even of
Victory, though this is a flight of fancy, for Nelson's association
with that ship was some years in the future). He enjoyed reading, though mainly the newspapers and naval books; Dampi-
er's *Voyages* was apparently a favourite. For Fanny there was
her needlework and watercolour painting.

Social pursuits were mainly family based and included
regular visits between the Rectory, the Boltons, the Matchams
and the William Nelsons. In December 1790 Nelson and Fanny
were invited to stay at Wolterton and spent several weeks there.
The Rector asked Kitty to buy Fanny a 'plain Hansom bonnett,
such as she may wear at Wolterton if need be'.[78] Visits to Wolterton became an annual event thereafter.

In April 1790 came some unwelcome naval business. Nelson went to the local horse fair one day and came back with
a 'Gallwey, a little pony'[79] (later to be named Tycho). On his
return he found that in his absence two men had arrived at the
Rectory and frightened Fanny by questioning her about her
identity and then pressing on her a document for him. It gave
notice of a court action some American captains were intending to take against him relating to his previous service in the
West Indies. Nelson was prepared to fight any such case, and in
the end it came to nothing, but he was outraged by the way the
men had acted and complained to the Admiralty.

Family business in 1789 seems to have involved financial problems for Thomas Bolton again, for in May Nelson was arranging, once again, for the payment of money into his account.

There were two deaths in the family during the year. Nelson's paternal grandmother, who had been looked after by William and Sarah at Hilborough, died aged 91 in July. Edmund was still at the Boltons', where his father thought he was becoming too much of a burden, and so in September he was moved to the rectory where Fanny was able to help his nurse, Dame Smith, look after him, but 'Poor Edmund declines very fast'[80] wrote his father, and later, 'Poor Edmund seems to drop so gradually it is scarce to be perceived. We hope he lives in no great pain.'[81] In December he finally died and it was Nelson who took charge of the funeral arrangements in great detail:

> *The hearse is to come from Fakenham at 10 o'clock to receive the body, which will be met at the church gate by Mr Crowe, who is ordered a scarf, hat-band and gloves. The body to be carried by the six oldest parishioners, who are to receive a crown a piece after the funeral and, instead of gloves, each man is to have a handkerchief for their wives of the same price.[82]*

The year saw joy as well, though, for Catherine Matcham gave birth to a boy, George, in November. The news was celebrated by the servants at Barton, who 'took the liberty of your garden With our guns, and fired 3 vollies'.[83]

In September 1790 the Rector decided to move from the rectory: 'I have hired one of the very small houses near [Burnham] Ulph church, which will lessen the fatigue of Sunday duty'.[84] He called it his 'town residence'. He also felt, no doubt, that Nelson and Fanny needed some privacy. Nelson was, he hoped, 'fixed at Thorpe, a place he delights in, but I wish it was a little better accommodated to Mrs N., as a woman who would sometimes choose a little variety'.[85]

In the Spring of 1791 the Matchams moved from Norfolk to settle in Hampshire, where they were building a house, Shepherd's Spring, near Ringwood. Their family now included a second son, Henry, who had been born in February. It must have made things quieter for Nelson who enjoyed the company of nephews and nieces. His social life, however, included a visit to the Lynn Feast that autumn, which he and Fanny enjoyed greatly. In December they were at Wolterton as usual and whilst they were there their distant relation, Lord Walpole of Houghton, died. Despite the fact that they had never had any social relationship with him they went into formal mourning, as propriety dictated. The Rector wrote to Catherine:

Statue of Capt. George Vancouver by the Purfleet, King's Lynn. Vancouver, Nelson's contemporary, sailed with Captain Cook and is famous for his own voyage of discovery in the north Pacific. He is celebrated as King's Lynn's most famous maritime son. Nelson was a west Norfolk man also but it may be that King's Lynn was upset by the stronger links he forged with Norwich.

> *We are in mourning the same as that family for a fortnight. You may with great propriety do the same. If any ask why? You may say that the late lord's grandfather, Sir R. Walpole and your great grandmother were sister and brother. So stands the consanguinity.[86]*

1792 saw the same mixture of domestic success and sadness. In October Nelson wrote to his sister Kitty to offer his sympathies on the death of little Henry Matcham, just 18 months old. On the positive side he was able to report that Suckling had just gone up to Cambridge where he was to study for the church at Christ's College. Happily, 'He is so attentive to his dutys . . . that we hear he is likely to acquit himself with

credit'.[87] Otherwise, this letter was as full as so many others with the trivia and gossip of family and local affairs, which Nelson nevertheless seems clearly to have enjoyed:

> *Mr B. [Thomas Bolton] has asked £1200 for Thorpe, but I can hardly think he will get it . . . Miss Crowe was at the Sessions ball at Norwich, and danced I understand with Lt. Suckling [a second cousin of Nelson] of the Artillery . . . Mr Robert Crowe drank tea here by himself last Wednesday, on purpose I believe to enquire of me about him & when he heard that he was likely to have one time or other £1500 a Year, he told us his sister danced all the evening with him (so we put these things together).*

Another letter in December revealed that he and Fanny had been at the last Aylsham Assembly. Such were their social horizons.

The Black Boys Inn, Aylsham. The Aylsham Assemblies were held here in Nelson's time.

Politics sometimes featured in Nelson's correspondence at this time. In November 1792 he wrote to the Duke of Clarence (whose friendship he had made when the latter was a midshipman in the West Indies) to express his concern about events in Norfolk:

> *Societies are formed . . . on principles certainly inimical to our present Constitution, both in Church and State . . . I have been staying some time with my relation Lord Walpole, near Norwich, at which place, and near it, the Clubs are supported by Members of the Corporation; and they avow that till some of the nobles and others in Parliament are served as they were in France, they will not be able to get their rights.*[88]

Typical of these societies was the Revolution Society, founded in Norwich in 1789 ostensibly to celebrate the centenary of the Glorious Revolution (the accession of William of Orange in 1688) but more interested in debating the ideas coming out of revolutionary France. A month later he was writing to the prince again:

> *Our lord Lieutenant has summoned a meeting of the Norfolk Justices on Tuesday next, the 11th; and I have no doubt that they will resolve to do collectively, what none of them chose to do individually – to take away the licenses from those public-houses who allow of improper Societies meeting at them, and to take up those incendiaries who go from ale-house to ale-house, advising the poor people to pay no taxes, etc.*[89]

He referred in particular to one of these radicals who had been active in the neighbourhood, a local clergyman named Joseph Priestley. Though his response was conservative his sympathies were, typically, with the labourers themselves, who were being 'seduced by promises and hopes of better times'. They were 're-ally in want of everything to make life comfortable' and much of the problem was the 'neglect of the Country Gentlemen, in not making their farmers raise their wages, in some small proportion, as the prices of necessaries increased'. To support this assertion he included with his letter 'An Account of the earnings and expenses of a labourer in Norfolk with a wife and three children'. It showed that they had 'not quite tuppence a day for each person; and to drink nothing but water, for beer our poor labourers never taste, unless they are tempted, which is too often the case, to go to the Alehouse'. He believed that, treated fairly, 'a want of loyalty is not among their faults'. Nelson was to extend this same consideration to his seamen, expecting and receiving the same loyalty.

In these letters to Prince William, Nelson was also look-ing for the Prince to use his influence in securing him a new command. This was the one theme which underlay the whole of Nelson's five years 'on the beach'. Despite his enjoyment of friends, family and farming he was desperate to get back to sea. The newspapers were devoured weekly for anything that signalled the possibility of action. A tradition at Burnham Overy Staithe recalls that 'on Saturday afternoons (publication day for the *Norfolk Chronicle*) Captain Nelson used to take his work down to the bank (the embankment between the mead-ows and salt marshes)'.[90] Perhaps this was the newspapers. Any significant news had him writing to anyone who might have some influence or going down in person to London to press his case at the Admiralty for a new command.

Then, in January 1793, war with France looked imminent

and Nelson went back to London to present himself at the Admiralty again. This time, as he wrote ecstatically to Fanny: '*Post nubile Phoebus:*- After clouds comes sunshine.'[91] The Admiralty had promised him a ship. He didn't forget though to ask her to 'Tell my father I had not forgot his hat, it is ordered'!

Back at Burnham, he did not have to wait long before receiving orders to commission the *Agamemnon* (64). News soon got about and it was not long before he was being pressed to take on the sons of his neighbours. The Rector noted that 'Severall men in and about the Burnhams are Entered for him'.[92] Amongst the midshipmen who joined him were three clergymen's sons, two from Norfolk and one from Suffolk: William, son of Rev. William Bolton of Hollesley in Suffolk, Susannah's brother-in-law; 12-year-old William, son of Dixon Hoste, Rector of Tittleshall, and John, son of Thomas Weath-

The harbour at Burnham Overy Staithe, where the young Horace would have first seen sea-going vessels, and where Captain Nelson is reputed to have taken his reading down to the bank.

erhead, Rector of Sedgeford. Messrs Hoste and Weatherhead had both asked Coke to recommend their sons. Assembling the rest of the crew was one of Nelson's duties and, preferring to recruit men he felt comfortable with, he arranged to send out 'a Lieutenant and four Midshipmen to get men at every Seaport in Norfolk, and to forward them to Lynn and Yarmouth'.[93] He also arranged with his old mentor Commodore Locker for the transfer to *Agamemnon* of Maurice Suckling (the son of his cousin, William Suckling of Woodton) who had been a midshipman with him on *Boreas*. Another former *Boreas* man he secured was the faithful Frank Lepee, again as captain's servant. The man who was eventually to replace Lepee also joined: 22-year-old Thomas Allen of Sculthorpe, who had been one of the family servants at Burnham. A late recruit was Thomas Withers of North Walsham who joined as schoolteacher for the young midshipmen.

During *Agamemnon's* subsequent service in the Mediterranean there were times when a large number of the crew were absent but Nelson is reported to have observed that those 'Agamemnons' he had were chiefly Norfolk men, and he always reckoned them as good as two others![94]

Before leaving Burnham, Nelson gave a farewell feast at the Plough (now the Lord Nelson) in the village. Whilst most of the men of the village were there, there were a group of boys outside, one of whom was the son of Mrs High (formerly Nurse Blackett at the Rectory). He had been upset at not being allowed in and had been teased by the others. A fight developed which Nelson observed. High, the younger and smaller, put up what Nelson described as 'a right valiant fight' earning him and his descendants the nickname 'Valiant' High.[95]

Nelson left Burnham on the morning of 4th February. He spent a month commissioning *Agamemnon* at Chatham and so was able to spend time with Uncle William and with the Matchams, who were on a visit to London and staying at Kentish Town. His stepson Josiah had expressed a desire to join the navy, and Nelson had been against it. He discussed with uncle William the idea of Josiah training for the law instead but realised that it would be too expensive. So Nelson suggested that Fanny should bring him up to London, 'For if he is to go, he must go with me'.[96]

In March Fanny brought Josiah down to Kentish Town and he went aboard *Agamemnon* as Midshipman. Getting Nelson's personal things from Norfolk proved to be trying. On 15th March he was complaining that they had still not sailed from Wells. They eventually left there on 30th April on a local ship, the *Supply,* but had not arrived at Sheerness ten days later. Five days later he was able to report that they had arrived safely, but without the key to his bureau drawers!

Brother Maurice visited him aboard at Spithead on 29th April and 'it blew so hard I could not land him, he conse-

The Lord Nelson, Burnham Thorpe. This was the Plough in Nelson's day and it was here that Nelson gave his farewell dinner for the villagers in 1793.

quently went to sea with me'![97] He managed to get back ashore six days later. Nelson finally left England bound for the Mediterranean on 11th May.

His going left a vacuum in Norfolk. Fanny did not want to live in the Rectory alone and after a couple of weeks

she moved out. She stayed awhile with the William Nelsons at Hilborough and William Suckling at Kentish Town, and in May she was at Ringwood where she helped the Matchams with their house-warming at Shepherd Springs. By August she had returned to Norfolk and taken lodgings at Swaffham. Fortunately she had recently received a small legacy on the death of her uncle, James Herbert, in Nevis, and so, as the Rector put it, 'Her income is now easy and independent'.[98] The Rector did not want to move back into the Rectory, nor did he want to let it, though he thought he might 'put in a Labourer'.[99] It was, however, used by Suckling when he was not at Cambridge, and 'The little farm and garden at Thorpe he takes great pleasure in'.[100] Nelson certainly did not want to lose it. He wrote to Fanny:

> I assure you it cannot give you more pleasure than it will me, for us to be settled again at Burnham and I sincerely hope our father will not part with the house to any one so as to prevent our getting into it again.[101]

St Vincent and Santa Cruz

FOR THE NEXT four years Nelson was in action in the Mediterranean, gradually making a name for himself; as he wrote to Fanny from Genoa in November 1795, 'Agamemnon is as well known throughout Europe as one of Mr Harwood's ships is at Overy'.[102] Throughout this period Nelson kept up a regular correspondence with his family, particularly his wife, his father and brother William, but also with sisters Susannah and Catherine, brothers Maurice and Suckling, and Uncle William Suckling. Nelson's letters were full of his own doings and those of the fleet and this news was passed on to the rest of the family and friends. Fewer letters survive from his family to Nelson but these were full of Burnham news and gossip. He wrote to Fanny, for example, in September 1795:

> *I have had a long letter from Suckling telling me all the Burnham news, which is all new to me and very pleasant to hear. For the moment I fancy myself at the old parsonage.*[103]

Suckling's progress, in fact, had continued to be a matter of concern for both his father and Nelson. He finally finished at Cambridge in the Autumn of 1794 and returned to Burnham as his father's curate. Brother William at this time had decided to purchase the Hilborough advowson from the rest of the family and so Nelson was called upon to help. His father wrote to Fanny in October 1794: 'he has done his part towards the negotiation for the advowson, I thank him'.[104]

One thing that worried Nelson at first was Fanny's inability to settle, for she was not happy at Swaffham. In July he wrote: 'I can hardly guess where this letter will find you but I hope

The Battle of St Vincent, in which Nelson was captain of the Captain. His actions, undertaken without orders, were instrumental in gaining the victory. (Engraving by Pickett after J. Clark, from Orme's Graphic History of . . . Nelson, *1806)*

you will get comfortable somewhere.'[105] She was soon off on another round of visits, to Hilborough, Wolterton, Ringwood, Bath, Bristol and Plymouth. By November 1794, however, she had settled at Bath with the Rector who was to make this increasingly his permanent home. He wrote to Kitty:

> *I begin to feel myself at Home . . . Mrs Nelson truly supplies a kind and watchful child over the infirmities and whimsies of age.*[106]

In his letters to Fanny, Nelson also sought to reassure her of his affection:

> *How I long for a letter from you. Next to being with you, it is the greatest pleasure I can receive.*[107]

In March 1794 he wrote:

> *I please myself much with the hopes of hearing you play on the pianoforte when we are snug at Burnham.*[108]

His nostalgia for Burnham and Norfolk was a constant theme during this period, especially at times of dissatisfaction and frustration when he would express his hope that the war would end and he could return. He was conscious of his lack of capital and his ambitions were suitably modest:

> *I hope to save my pay which with a little addition will buy us a little cottage where I shall be as happy as in a house as large as Holkham.*

It was always 'a peaceful cottage in Norfolk'[109] that he visualised, perhaps with a bit of land (like the rectory). Indeed in August 1795 he remarked: 'A little farm and my good name is all my wants or wishes.'[110]

Nelson's letters to his wife also reassured her about her son – 'he is a real good boy and most affectionately loves me'. Josiah would often enclose a letter of his own or just add a brief postscript to one of Nelson's. Nelson took his responsibilities to Josiah and his other serving relatives seriously. He was able to report to Fanny in March 1794, 'You will be glad to hear that Suckling is made a lieutenant'. He treated his other Norfolk midshipmen almost like family. He clearly enjoyed their company and took pride in their development and they were often mentioned in his letters, with instructions to pass on their news to their families. 'Suckling has been very ill but is out of danger. Bolton, Hoste and Weatherhead are recovered.'[111] On occasion they accompanied him on excursions ashore: 'Josiah, myself and Hoste go tomorrow to Pisa for to spend the day.'[112] Hoste he seems to have taken a particular interest in:

> *I am glad the Hostes seem sensible of my attention to their son but he is indeed a most exceeding good boy, and will shine in our service.*[113]

In February 1794 Nelson felt moved to write to Rev. Dixon Hoste:

> *You cannot receive much more pleasure in reading this letter than I have in writing it, to say, that your Son is everything which his dearest friends can wish him to be.*[114]

Writing again in May he declared:

> *He highly deserves every thing I can do to make him happy . . . I love him; therefore shall say no more on that subject.*[115]

Nelson had a reputation for looking after the welfare of his

Key to the Large Print & Picture of ADM.ᵉ NELSON'S Boarding the Spanish Ships &

Lᵈ Sᵗ VINCENT.   VICTORY.

N.º 1, Capt Berry.
2, Admᵗ Nelson.
3, Capt Noble.
4, Lieut Pearson 69 Regt
5, Lieut Withers.
6, O.Brien a Spanish Priest.
7, Capt P. Spicer.
8, Lieut Jos.ᵃ Nesbit.
9, Capt Miller.
10, Soldier of the 69ᵗʰ
11, Harvey, an English Sailor
12, Hooper, the Sailor who Struck, the Spanish
13, Ramsay, one of the Admirals Barge men
14, a Spanish Sailor.
15, Zenace Tore, the first Lieut Spanish
16, Don Francisco Xavier Winthuysen, the Spanish
17, Don Tomas D'khnnena, the Spanish

ordinary seamen as well. By late 1794, however, the behaviour of his servant Frank Lepee was becoming a trial. In November Nelson wrote to Fanny that 'his [Lepee's] mind is evidently deranged'.[116] By December he had had to replace him, but the replacement was so bad that he had been dismissed and Nelson now had 'only a Norfolk ploughman'.[117] Perhaps this was Tom Allen, for it was he who was to look after Nelson from then until Trafalgar.

On 14th February 1797 Nelson had, at last, the opportunity to distinguish himself in a major fleet battle at St Vincent. As captain of *Captain* (74) under Admiral Jervis, he played a major role in the ensuing victory. It was a stunning one, achieved principally through his own initiative, combined with a typical degree of recklessness and bravery. He wrote to Fanny enclosing '*A few remarks relative to myself in the* Captain' which included:

ST VINCENT AND
SANTA CRUZ

*OPPOSITE: Nelson,
Captain Berry, officers
and crew of the*
Captain *at St Vincent,
from Orme's* Graphic
History of . . . Nelson,
1806.

*BELOW: Nelson's
actions in closing with
the Spanish ships* San
Nicolas *and* San Josef,
*and boarding them,
ensured victory at the
battle of St Vincent.
(Print after T. C.
Moore, from the* Boys'
Own Paper *1886)*

There is a saying in the fleet too flattering for me to omit telling. – viz. 'Nelson's Patent Bridge for boarding first rates'.[118]

He repeated this to his uncle, William Suckling, writing that 'you will receive pleasure from the share I had in making it a most brilliant day'.[119] He did not forget, however, to send his congratulations on the marriage of Suckling's daughter, news of which he had only just received.

Nelson's official reward for his part in the victory was the Order of the Bath, but he enjoyed more the public fame which ensued and which quite overwhelmed his father. By the ordinary course of events he was also, in February, promoted to flag rank as Rear-Admiral of the Blue. Fanny wrote to him: 'I never saw anything elevate our father equal to this. He repeated with pleasure the last words: "His good uncle (Capt. Maurice Suckling) told him that he would live to see you an Admiral."'[120]

For the new knight a suitable coat of arms was required and Nelson enjoyed designing this, sending the details to brother Maurice whom he asked to negotiate the details with the York Herald. Brother William came up with a Latin motto which Nelson turned into English as '*Faith and Works*'.

Musing on other ways to celebrate his triumph, Nelson had written to Fanny a week after the battle,

I have some thoughts of sending the Spanish admiral's sword to be hung up in the Guild Hall at Norwich if it will be acceptable.[121]

A few days later he wrote to William Windham, MP for Norwich (in Nicolas the letter is addressed to 'Wadham' Windham), to ask if he thought the City would accept it, as

I know no place where it would give me or my family more pleasure to have it kept, than in the capital City of the County in which I had the honour to be born.[122]

With it he sent the sword in a box and the following letter to the Mayor of Norwich:

Having the good fortune on the most glorious 14th of February, to become possessed of the Sword of the Spanish Rear Admiral Don Xavier Francisco Winthuysen . . . and being born in the County of Norfolk, I beg leave to present the Sword to the City of Norwich in order to its being preserved as a Memento of the Event, and of my Affection for my Native County.[123]

This 'Nelson Monument' was made by John Ninham to house the St Vincent sword which Nelson presented to Norwich in 1797. The monument was later embellished with a crocodile to commemorate the Nile and then a plaque to commemorate Trafalgar. Formerly in the Regalia Room at the Guildhall, the monument is now in the Castle Museum.

The sword was duly received at the city's Quarterly Assembly in May 1797 and the Assembly promptly elected Nelson an Honorary Freeman of the City. Brother Maurice wrote to Fanny: 'I understand Lynn will follow the example . . . and that they wish the sword had been presented to them'.[124] Perhaps it was this imagined slight which put paid to any hope of such an honour, as brother William wrote in October: 'Nothing was done at Lynn at the feast, and I rather believe the Corporation is divided, and they say they have their reasons'.[125] Nevertheless he did receive a number of other honorary freedoms, including those of Bath, London and Bristol.

Nelson had often, when he was able, sent presents home for his family and friends. In June 1796, for example he wrote to Fanny:

> *I have sent my small present for you . . . The black silk stockings I mean for my father if he chooses. If he takes only a part, give my brother Suckling two pair.*[126]

Burnham did not escape his generosity either. In 1795 he sent £200 to his father as a winter gift for the poor of the village. After St Vincent, however, his gifts became a little grander, in keeping with his enhanced social station. In May 1797 he was intending to send to Fanny 'some Naples sashes . . . and a gown also 5 elegant drawings of the action [St Vincent] when opportunity offers'.[127] His winter gift to the Burnham poor that year was to be 'fifty good large blankets with the letter N wove in the centre that they may not be sold'.[128] He hoped that 'they will last some person or other for seven years at least'.

His desire for a Norfolk cottage was not forgotten, though it would still have to be a modest one. A large number of houses were seen or considered as Fanny and the rest of the family searched for a suitable property, including a house in the Upper Close in Norwich and another one eight miles south of the city; also 'Mr. Hogges' house' in Aylsham, and even a 'very poor farm house and old outbuildings'[129] with 100 acres (40 hectares) near Pickenham. Even Shepherd's Spring, the Matchams' house in Hampshire, was suggested but Nelson wrote to Fanny, 'if you do not object I should like Norfolk in preference to any other part of the kingdom'.[130]

On 24th July 1797 Nelson was wounded in an abortive attempt on the port of Santa Cruz on Tenerife in the Canary Islands. His right arm had to be amputated as a result. Although his subsequent letter to Fanny (his first to her written with his left hand) made light of his injuries, he was uncertain of his future in the navy and felt that 'the cottage is now more necessary than ever'.[131]

Nelson returned to England on 1st September to convalesce and was reunited with his father and Fanny at Bath. He did intend to visit Norfolk and wrote to brother William: 'I may visit Norfolk for a few days, especially if a decent house is likely to be met with near Norwich: but Wroxham very far indeed exceeds my purse.'[132] Another reason to visit Norfolk came with an invitation from the Norwich Corporation, which he accepted, to attend on Lord Mayor's Day to receive his Freedom of the City in person.

In the event, however, Nelson did not manage to visit Norfolk. His wound gave him much pain but there was also business to deal with and engagements to attend. Most of Nelson's brief stay in England, therefore, was spent in Bath or London.

One of his less happy duties was to write to Rev. Thomas Weatherhead at Sedgeford in Norfolk to offer his condolences on the death of his son John who had fallen at Tenerife: 'Believe me, I have largely partaken in our real cause for grief in the loss of a most excellent young man.'[133]

Family matters also occupied him now that fame and a knighthood had given him increased influence. In October 1797 his father formally resigned his Burnham living. His hope was that it could be secured for Suckling and so Nelson was enlisted to write to the Lord Chancellor to request this. The request was granted, much to everyone's relief for it effectively secured Suckling's future although his father's expectations of him were low: 'He will pass (no Doubt) among a Crowd of undistinguished preachers, and gain some respect in the village of his Residence from his quiet disposition, his liking to a little conviviality, and his passion for Grey-Hounds and Coursing.'[134]

Brother William, of course, had ambitions which he also thought his brother could further. He had his eye on a possible vacancy at Norwich cathedral and wrote to Nelson that someone had assured him that 'he knew as a fixed and certain thing that you had secured the vacant stall for me, and that the Lord Chancellor had promised it to me and all was settled; I thought your bows to the Great Seal would produce something.'[135] Unhappily the post did not become vacant so, looking instead for a similar post at any cathedral, he pressed Nelson to 'Pray continue your bows to the Great Seal. Who knows what may happen now the iron is hot'. Obliging as ever, Nelson wrote to the Lord Chancellor again about his brother's wish adding that 'any Residentiary Stall will be acceptable, the nearer Norfolk the more agreeable'.[136] It was not until 1803 that William eventually got a stall, as a prebendary of Canterbury cathedral.

On 25th September 1797 Nelson went to St James's Palace for his investiture with the Order of the Bath. With him he took two guests. One was William. The other was Edward Berry. Berry had been born in Norwich in 1768 and, like Nelson, had been educated at the Grammar School. He first met Nelson when he was appointed Lieutenant on *Captain* and he soon proved to be a man after Nelson's own heart. He was aboard *Captain* at St Vincent and led the first party to board the Spanish *San Nicolas*, Nelson leading the other. The two had become firm friends. When Nelson was introduced to the King the monarch exclaimed, 'You have lost your right arm!' to which Nelson's instant response was, 'But not my right hand, as I have the honour of presenting Captain Berry'.[137] A few weeks later Berry announced his engagement to his cousin Louisa, daughter of Dr Samuel Forster, the headmaster of Norwich Grammar School, and Nelson wrote to him at Norwich on 28th November to 'most heartily congratulate you on becoming one of us'.[138] In his letter to Berry, Nelson also took the opportunity to enclose, for the Mayor, a drawing of his coat of arms so that these could be included in the monument which the Corporation had ordered from John Ninham in November to house the St Vincent sword. The monument was later altered after the battles of the Nile and Trafalgar to record those events.

Berry on board Nelson's ship at St Vincent, where he was the first man to board the Spanish ship San Nicolas, *closely followed by Nelson. From Orme's* Graphic History of . . . Nelson, *1806.*

It was in November that Nelson and Fanny finally saw a suitable house. It was found for them through sister Susannah by her brother-in-law Sam Bolton. Named Roundwood, it offered all they had been looking for. It comprised a four-bedroomed house with barn, stables, cowhouse and other outbuildings, in 50 acres (20 hectares) of land. Importantly, Nelson was able to acquire it for £2,000, exactly the sum he had felt he could afford. The one original stipulation that it did not meet was that it was not in Norfolk; the house was near Sam Bolton, a few miles from Ipswich. Nevertheless Nelson signed the agreement that month. As it had a sitting tenant they had to wait until May the following year before they could take possession. In the event Nelson was back at sea by then and was never to live there though Fanny and his father did so.

On 8th December Nelson had to write to Berry again to warn that 'If you mean to marry, I would recommend your doing it speedily, or the to be Mrs Berry will have little of your company'.[139] Their new ship was likely to be ready soon. The couple married at Norwich on 12th December.

There was a last family gathering for the Nelsons at Bath in January 1798. Nelson was in better health and the party in good spirits. He had been having some trouble with bureaucracy, the authorities insisting on a formal certificate before allowing a pension for the loss of his sight in the right eye. Nelson's response had been that they might as well expect one to prove the loss of his arm and the family, enjoying the absurdity of that idea, decided to draw up their own. Written, it would appear, by William and Catherine, it began, 'Whereas your humble Petitioner has had the misfortune to lose his

Brother in His Majesty's Service, & is now obliged to do all his Master's work himself' and was signed 'Admiral Nelson's left hand'.[140]

The Nile

ON 29TH MARCH 1798 Nelson went aboard his new ship, *Vanguard* (74), with Berry as his Captain and they set sail for the Mediterranean three days later. His squadron was given the task of keeping watch on the French fleet at Toulon where a large scale expedition was clearly in preparation. When the French left port under cover of a gale Nelson searched for them across the Mediterranean with an increasing sense of anxiety until he caught them at anchor in Aboukir Bay, near the mouth

A naval cannon of Nelson's period. Now in Yarmouth market place, it was discovered near the former Naval Arsenal in Southtown.

of the Nile. The battle which followed was the most destructive of the war. Virtually the whole of the enemy fleet was either destroyed or taken.

The response to this victory, especially at home where fears of invasion had been in the air, was ecstatic. Word was that his country would elevate him to the peerage so brother William wrote to him in mid-October to pass on their father's reminder that the title of Orford was now extinct (this would demonstrate Nelson's Walpole connection.) He was also excited by the prospect that 'Parliament will settle the same pension upon yourself and the next two possessors of the title [i.e. including himself] which they have done upon Earl St Vincent and Viscount Duncan'.[141] Indeed the newspapers were suggesting that 'His majesty has intimated to his ministers that he expects some dignitary should be given to the father and brother of the gallant Lord Nelson, who are both in the church'.[142]

In the event Nelson was created a baron and chose the title Baron Nelson of the Nile and of Burnham Thorpe. Writing to Lord Hood in early October, Fanny had been sure that 'His unbounded affection for his father would make him wish to have it Baron Nelson'.[143] There were those, however, who felt that a barony was an insult, after the rewards that Jervis and Duncan had received for their victories. Brother Maurice was particularly indignant. When Evan Nepean, Secretary to the Admiralty, called him in to inform him of the honour, 'He was so hurt, and surprised, that he never made any reply'.[144] He wrote to Fanny that 'I am by no means satisfied with it, and if I had been authorized I should have rejected it with contempt'.[145] Writing again the following day he considered the question of the succession to the title and declared 'that William may have

A page of sketches depicting men present at the battle of the Nile; Berry is shown at the top of the group as Captain of Vanguard, Nelson's flagship. (From Orme's Graphic History of . . . Nelson, 1806)

N.º 1 Lord Nelson.
2 Sir Edwd Berry.
3 Mid.ⁿ Prebie. Son of Ld Carysfort.
4 Lt Adye.
5 Mid. Ives
6 Mid. Collier Son of the late Sr Geo. Collier.
7 Lt Compton.
8 Lt Galway first Lieu.^t of the Vanguard.
9 Garrett Grehin.
10 Andersen one of the Marines.
11 Hobdy a Seaman.

all the honours to himself. It will be my wish and request to my brother not to put my name in the patent.'

In the event only Nelson and his heirs were included and no rewards, financial or otherwise, were forthcoming for his family. Nelson himself, however, received a pension of £2,000 a year with his peerage and a host of other honours and awards, both British and foreign. Among those of local interest were the freedom of Thetford (presented in an oak box with a mounted silver inscription) and the freedom of Ipswich.

Nelson's name was fêted across the country and a flood of Nelson memorabilia was soon on sale to meet a huge popular demand. Thanksgiving services and celebratory festivals were organised, not least in his native county. The news reached Norwich on 2nd October whereupon the bells of St Peter Mancroft were rung all day. Upon receipt of the news at Dereham a troop of the Norfolk Yeomanry were received in the town by a band playing patriotic songs and fired three volleys for the benefit of the crowd of spectators.

In Suffolk, where Fanny was now living at Roundwood, news of the victory prompted Ipswich immediately to vote Nelson the Freedom of the Borough, and on 8th October Fanny attended a grand commemorative ball at the Assembly Rooms there, accompanied by Nelson's father and Berry's sister.

On 9th October Mr and Mrs John Berry gave a grand Ball in honour of Nelson and their brother Edward at the Assembly House in Norwich. The guests included the Mayor and Mayoress, Lord and Lady Walpole and Captain Berry's wife. Centrepiece of the decorations was a painting of a naval column ornamented with trophies and inscribed 'NELSON. BERRY. VICTORY.' Other decorations included the inscription 'Health

and long life to the Norfolk Hero' and the toasts included one
to 'Mrs Edward Berry, and may our gallant admiral long retain
his right hand'.[146]

Later, when official news of the victory reached Norwich,
the church bells were rung again and the Union flag was hung
above the French tricolour from the tower of St Peter Mancroft. The corporation sent a message of congratulations to the
king and resolved to ask Nelson to sit for a civic portrait. The
29th November was designated an official day of thanksgiving
and saw the Mayor, Aldermen and Sheriffs of Norwich proceed
to the cathedral with the volunteer corps for a thanksgiving
service. Afterwards an ox was roasted in the market place. In
the evening many buildings were lighted, over 50 houses being
decorated with illuminated transparencies depicting patriotic
themes.

In Great Yarmouth, Admiral Duncan (victor of the battle

The Assembly House,
Norwich

of Camperdown in 1797 and then in command of the North Sea fleet) gave a dinner at the Duke's Head Inn where the guests included the Russian Admiral Mackaroff and the captains from his ships then in the Roads.

At Swaffham the town celebrated 'in a universal blaze' and the Town Hall, Assembly Rooms, church and various houses were decorated. A grand ball at the Assembly Rooms was attended by the Boltons and the William Nelsons (William wrote to Nelson that his wife had 'sent for a dress for the occasion'[147]). At Burnham Thorpe the Nelsons' old friend, Sir Mordaunt Martin, organised a celebratory dinner for the poor, entertained by the Burnham Ulph band, and he opened a subscription for the relief of the families of those killed or wounded in the battle.

Nationally there was a proposal to build a monument in honour of the recent naval victories, and one 'Blakeney' submitted a suitable design for one to the *Gentleman's Magazine* in 1799. It was for 'a noble mansion-house to be erected for Lord Nelson, on a rising ground a little to the south-west of Burnham-Market in Norfolk'. Sadly nothing further came of it.

Naples

NAPLES HAD BEEN Nelson's destination after the battle of the Nile and there he was immediately overwhelmed by the adoring attentions of the Neapolitans, but more particularly by those of Lady Hamilton. He soon found himself involved in Neapolitan politics, and his loyalties to both wife and country

Plan of a MANSION HOUSE, proposed for Lord NELSON.

A mansion proposed to be built for Nelson to celebrate his victory at the Nile. From a letter to the Gentleman's Magazine, *1799*

were severely tested as he fell under the spell of Emma Hamilton and what he felt were his obligations to the Neapolitan court. Lord Minto, ambassador at Vienna, wrote to his wife, 'he does not seem at all conscious of the discredit he has fallen into, or the cause of it'.[148] Nelson himself found the atmosphere corrupting and confusing. In a letter to St Vincent he described Naples as 'a country of fiddlers and poets, whores and scoundrels'.[149]

During this period there was one comforting, though often irritating, reminder of home for Nelson in the form of the ever faithful Tom Allen. Allen had a knack for plain speaking which Nelson appreciated even though it sometimes embarrassed him. In February 1799 Nelson had an anniversary dinner aboard to celebrate the battle of St Vincent. During the meal Allen, with scant regard to etiquette, addressed one of the guests, a frigate captain, to ask about one of his friends who was aboard the captain's ship. The captain was speechless and an exasperated Nelson ordered Allen out, explaining:

> I really must get rid of that impudent lubber. I have often threatened, but somehow he contrives to defeat my firm intentions – he is faithful, honest, and attached, with great shrewdness mixed with his simplicity, which is unbounded. He was badly wounded in the action we are assembled to commemorate, nursed me tenderly at Santa Cruz, and is a townsman (i.e. from the same village). I mention these things . . . in palliation of his freedom.[150]

For Nelson loyalty was the most important of values and Allen was devoted to him. Indeed, within minutes he was back to remind his master that 'You will be ill if you takes any more wine'. Replying, 'You are perfectly right, Tom, and I thank you for the hint,' Nelson made his excuses before retiring. Allen continued to demonstrate a refreshing Norfolk bluntness which must have helped alleviate the artificialities of Neapolitan society. On 10th July 1799 the King of Naples came aboard the *Foudroyant* in Naples bay to be received by Nelson and his officers. When Allen was offered the King's hand to kiss he gave it 'a truly Norfolk shake . . . and a coarse growl of 'I hope you are well, Muster King. How do you do Muster King?'[151]

There was plenty of family news from home, principally from Fanny but also from William, from his father and his other brothers and sisters, but the volume of work his business occasioned made it difficult for him to respond as regularly. To William he wrote in April 1799:

> *You must not, nor any of my friends think, that because my letters are scarce and short that in any way they are forgot: the wonder even to me is, that I am able to write what I do.*[152]

Whilst in Naples in 1798, Nelson sat for a bust by Anne Seymour Damer. The original bust is now in the Guildhall, London; this engraving of it by James Godby comes from Orme's Graphic History of . . . Nelson, *1806.*

In August he wrote to Fanny: 'My dear father must forgive my not writing so often as I ought, and so must my brothers, sisters and friends'.[153] Letters from home were always welcome. In April 1799 he received letters from brother William and from his nephew Horatio (whom he called Horace) and niece Charlotte. William's news included that of the death of their uncle William Suckling (on 15th December 1798); he left Nelson a legacy of £100 and appointed him an executor. Otherwise, William was still grumbling about the lack of official recognition accorded to the family. Nelson had clearly been trying to do what he could, replying:

> *I feel that you have just cause for complaint that not one relation of the Victor of the Nile has been noticed. I wrote to both Mr Pitt and Mr Wyndham.*[154]

Neither, however, had answered. He had also tried what he could to advance brother Maurice, writing to Lord Spencer at the Admiralty, but 'the latter has told me he does not know how he can be useful to my brother Maurice'. Nevertheless Nelson assured William that 'Whenever [I can] in ANY way be useful to you or my nephew and niece, you know me not to be disinclined.' Writing in June 1799, Fanny brought him up to date with all the family news including, of course, their various financial problems. The Boltons had moved to Cranwich near Brandon, taking a farm that seems to have been more expensive than they could manage and about which tongues were wagging locally. The gossip was, however, that Thomas Bolton had 'a brother-in-law a great lord [i.e. Nelson], that is to pay all his debts, therefore he will be trusted'.[155] His father was troubled by 'the various passions that torment the Rector' (brother William), which included 'ambition, pride and a selfish disposition'. William's pride was particularly hurt by the Boltons' situation. His father was worried also by the bills he was expecting at Burnham, and for Fanny: 'My expenses are very great, entirely owing to the dearness of every article of life.'

Amongst the rewards Nelson had received after the Nile was an award of £10,000 from the East India Company. He was relieved that it allowed him to help his importunate relatives.

He clearly had a soft spot for Thomas Bolton. Fanny seems to have advanced him some money and Nelson wrote in July to say, 'I rejoice that you gave Mr Bolton the money and I wish it made up £500'. As for the East India Company grant: 'I beg that £2000 of it may be disposed of in the following manner; – £500 to be made up to Mr Bolton, and let it be a *God-send,* without any restriction; five hundred to Maurice, and five hundred to William. And if you think my sister Matcham would be gratified by it, do the same for her.' He reassured them that 'If I were rich I would do more', but made sure they appreciated that 'It will very soon be known how poor I am'.

Fanny's news had included that of brother Suckling's death in April, though Nelson took it philosophically: 'I am not surprised at my brother's death; three are now dead, younger than myself.'[156]

In August 1799 Fanny reported that she and his father had dined at Holkham where 'the Cokes were very attentive'.[157] In November she wrote of William's wish for her to 'give Mr Windham [MP for Norwich and Secretary of State for War] a gentle hint that nothing was done for the Nelson family.'[158] Although Nelson never seems to have found anything excessive in William's demands, his father did and, on this occasion, 'was hurt that William was so pressing and dissatisfied'. In March 1800 Fanny could not resist telling Nelson 'a profound secret . . . our good father is sitting for his picture', even though 'the picture is for you'.[159] The artist was Sir William Beechey, one of the most fashionable portrait painters of the day and an appropriate choice. Between 1782 and 1787 he had lived in Norwich where he had painted a number of civic portraits and in 1793 he had married a Norwich woman, Anne Phyllis Jessup. Fanny had visited Beechey to see his work and ask if he was able to visit an invalid. Sir William had said that 'really he never went to any person excepting the King and Royal family . . . but Madam may I ask who is the gentleman?'. On hearing that it was Nelson's father he had replied, 'My God, I would go to York to do it, yes madam directly'.[160]

The Wrestlers Inn in the Market Place was Yarmouth's premier inn. Nelson stayed here with Sir William and Lady Hamilton in 1800. Sir Hyde Parker was staying here before Copenhagen and James Sharman, first custodian of Nelson's Monument in the town, originally worked as a stable lad here. It was rebuilt in 1945 after damage by enemy action.

Return to England

IN MARCH 1800 Sir William Hamilton learned that he was to be replaced and would be returning to England. Nelson also had been ordered home and he decided to join them. The party travelled overland through Austria and Germany before arriving at Hamburg on 21st October 1800. The party included Nelson, Sir William and Lady Hamilton, Mrs Cadogan (Emma's mother), Miss Cornelia Knight (a friend of the Hamiltons'), Fatima (Emma's Egyptian maid) and, of course, Tom Allen. Nelson had hoped that a frigate might be provided to carry them to England but instead he had to hire one of the mail packets then sailing between Cuxhaven (Hamburg's outport) and Great Yarmouth. The party left on the *King George* (Captain Dean) on Friday 31st October having embarked at Oevelgoenne, five miles downstream from Hamburg, instead of at Cuxhaven, because of a threatened kidnap plot.

Their crossing took five days in bad weather but they eventually arrived in Yarmouth Roads on 6th November. Part of the North Sea fleet was in the Roads at the time, including, coincidentally, two of Nelson's former ships, *Raisonable* and *Agamemnon*. The party came ashore at Gorleston and took a carriage into Great Yarmouth, intending to stay at the Wrestlers Inn in the Market Place. The whole town was soon aware of Nelson's arrival and at the Haven Bridge an enthusiastic crowd took the horses from the carriage and drew it by hand to the inn. It was from an upper window there that Nelson addressed the crowd to proclaim that he was a Norfolk man and gloried in being so.

Nelson had little free time in Yarmouth. Admiral Dickson, commander of the North Sea Fleet, soon arrived to pay his respects accompanied by Captain Moss of the *Monarch*. The Vicar, Rev. Richard Turner, was another early visitor. At 2 p.m. the Mayor, Samuel Barker, and the Corporation arrived to present Nelson with the Freedom of the Borough. When Nelson put his left hand on the Bible to swear the oath, the Town Clerk,

The Return of the Hero: oil on canvas by Fred Roe, c. 1909, purporting to show Nelson's arrival at Yarmouth jetty on his return to England in November 1800. The Mayor, Town Clerk and municipal officers are there to present him with the Freedom of the Borough and Sir William and Lady Hamilton can be seen in the left foreground. In fact Nelson and his party landed at Gorleston, and the Freedom was presented later at the Wrestlers Inn.

Mr Watson, prompted; 'Your right hand, my lord' to which Nelson's amused reply was: 'That is at Tenerife'![161]

Throughout the day the town was *en fête* with bells ringing and ships in harbour flying their colours. In the evening the mayor was back, this time with the Yarmouth Loyal Volunteer corps of which he was the commander. Nelson spent an hour talking to them, mainly about the Nile and the bravery of his captains there. For the rest of the evening the infantry paraded and fired *feux de joie* while their band played, the crowds not dispersing until after midnight.

In the morning Nelson and his party attended church accompanied by the Mayor and Aldermen, entering to 'See the Conquering Hero Comes' on the organ. Taking their places under the west window they heard Mr Turner preach a sermon, taking as his text Proverbs 1:7, 'The fear of the Lord is the beginning of knowledge'. After the service Nelson dined with the Mayor at his house (on King Street between Rows 73 and 74) where he was provided with 'a most sumptuous and elegant cold collation'. On leaving he 'intimated an intention of visiting Yarmouth with Lady Nelson in the summer, should his country dispense with his services'.[162] It was a surprising remark in view of what was soon to happen but was, no doubt, only the expected courtesy in such a situation. Nelson's party left Great Yarmouth at three o'clock that afternoon and were escorted as far as Lowestoft by the Yarmouth Volunteer Cavalry under Lieut. William Palgrave. During their brief stay in Yarmouth there had been time for a few other duties. Conscious of a likely popular demand for recent pictures of Nelson, arrangements were made for a local artist, Matthew Keymer, to copy a portrait by the Palermo artist Leonardo Guzzardi,

When they landed at Yarmouth in November 1800, the Hamiltons had with them a portrait of Nelson by the Palermo artist Leonardo Guzzardi. It was copied by local artist Matthew Keymer and this print was taken from the copy and published in December.

which the Hamiltons had with them. Eight days later Keymer's copy was on show and orders were being taken for mezzotint engravings by the London engraver John Young. The print was published on 8th December. At the Wrestlers, the landlady, Mrs Suckling (whose husband claimed some relationship to Nelson), asked for permission to rename her hotel the Nelson Arms. Nelson's joking reply was, 'That would be absurd seeing that I have but one',[163] so the inn was renamed the Nelson Hotel instead. Finally Nelson arranged for his bankers to pay via Mr Warmington (the Navy Agent at Great Yarmouth and agent for the Cuxhaven packets) 5 guineas for the Town Clerk, 1 guinea for the Mayor's Officer and £50 for the Mayor to distribute to the needy in the town.

Within three months Nelson was back in Great Yarmouth, but this time on service. Much had happened in between, however. In London he had sat, at last, for Sir William Beechey for the portrait commissioned by the City of Norwich. The sittings seem to have been an enjoyable experience. No doubt Norfolk was a common bond between the two men and a friendship was established which was sealed by Nelson's gift to Beechey of the cocked hat which he had worn at the Nile and by Nelson becoming godfather to Beechey's son, Charles. The finished work, a full-length portrait, is probably the most heroic of Nelson's portraits. It was exhibited at the Royal Academy in May 1801 and delivered to Norwich in the Autumn, where it now hangs in Blackfriars Hall.

Nelson's private life was more problematical. On his way from Great Yarmouth to London Nelson had stopped briefly at Bamford's hotel in Ipswich and had visited his house at Roundwood. The house, however, was empty. Fanny was wait-

Beechey's portrait is reproduced on page 2 of this book.

ing for him in London and their uncomfortable reunion was there. Late in January 1801 his daughter Horatia was born to Lady Hamilton, an event which, though it had to be kept secret, made a separation from Fanny inevitable. Though he assured Fanny that 'there is nothing in you, or your conduct, I wish otherwise',[164] nevertheless he had determined that they should separate. In March he wrote from the *St George* at sea to inform her that 'my only wish is to be left to myself and wishing you every happiness'.[165] An astonished Fanny endorsed it 'this is my Lord Nelson's letter of dismissal' and sent it to brother Maurice for advice. His reply was that she should 'not take the least notice of it, as his brother seemed to have forgot himself'. But Nelson was serious and had made financial arrangements for their separate lives, which he spelled out in a memorandum: 'Lord Nelson has directed Mr Davison to pay every bill and expense of his and Lady Nelson's to the day of leaving London.'[166] Fanny was now to have £2,000 a year (payable in quarterly instalments) plus a lump sum of £4,000. Nelson had also made his final effort on behalf of his stepson, arranging for Josiah to have a new command: 'I have done *all* for him and he may again as he has often done before wish me to break my neck … but I have done my duty.' It was a far cry from the time after his injury at Tenerife when he had written to Fanny that 'Josiah … was principally instrumental in saving my life'.[167] Since then, however, Josiah had disappointed him as a captain and had grown increasingly antipathetic to his stepfather as he watched and heard accounts of Nelson's developing relationship with Lady Hamilton. In the event Josiah never got a new ship and soon left the navy.

OPPOSITE: Nelson sat for this portrait by local artist Matthew Keymer at Yarmouth in 1800 whilst waiting for his fleet to sail to the Baltic.

ENGLAND EXPECTS EVERY MAN TO DO HIS DUTY

The Baltic

AS HE APPROACHED Yarmouth on 6th March Nelson
wrote to Emma: 'In sight of Yarmouth. With what different
sensations to what I saw it before! Then I was with all I hold
dear in the world; now . . . how indifferent to the approach.'[168]
The reference was, of course, to his arrival with the Hamiltons
the previous year. Having arrived, however, he was determined
to get on with his new task. Unfortunately this was more than
can be said for his commander, Admiral Sir Hyde Parker. Parker had been given command of the North Sea fleet at Great
Yarmouth, charged with the task of persuading the Danes to
withdraw from a hostile alliance with Russia and Sweden.
Staying at the Nelson Hotel, however, he was finding excuses
for delaying his departure whilst planning a grand ball for his
new young wife. 'Consider how nice it must be laying in bed
with a young wife, compared to a damned cold, raw wind'[169]
was Nelson's caustic remark. He called on Parker at the hotel at
eight in the morning, 'choosing to be amusingly exact to that
hour, which he considered as a very late one for business',[170] as
his friend Colonel Stewart recalled, and was infuriated by the
resulting interview which was brief and formal with no discus-
sion of their mission nor any orders. A frustrated letter to his
friend Troubridge at the Admiralty had the desired effect, however, and Parker soon received a personal letter from the First

Lord, St Vincent, to the effect that his reputation would suffer if he remained at Great Yarmouth any longer. Parker cancelled his ball, sent his wife home and prepared for sea. The fleet finally sailed on the 12th.

Posterity benefited from Nelson's enforced delay, for it allowed the artist Keymer to approach him for permission to paint his portrait. Some of the resultant sittings were held at the Wrestlers and were witnessed by a local jeweller, Samuel Aldred, who 'continued to speak of this unforgettable experience to the end of his days'.[171] Keymer's portrait was presented, after Trafalgar, to the Society of Friends, a local convivial club, and they provided it with the ornate frame, incorporating cannon and wreaths, which it still has. A year or so later the Friends disbanded and the portrait was acquired by Great Yarmouth Corporation and hung in the Town Hall. It is now on show at the Norfolk Nelson Museum in the town.

Nelson's stay at Great Yarmouth also allowed him to catch up with some local correspondence. He wrote to Berry regarding a new scheme for directing guns and suggested that he might like to visit him, sending his respects to 'Doctor Forster [Berry's father-in-law] and all my friends in Norwich'.[172] He replied to an outstanding letter from a Mr Pillans in Norwich who had written to inform him 'that the Ancient Order of Gregorians [at Norwich] had elected me a Member' and he returned 'my thanks for the great honour they have been pleased to confer on me'.[173] The Gregorians were a convivial society originally founded in London. The Norwich branch boasted many of the county's leading men as members and met in their own chapter room in the White Swan Inn near St Peter Mancroft.

Parker's direction of the Copenhagen campaign was as cautious as his preparations at Great Yarmouth had been protracted and it was Nelson's typically robust approach which secured victory. The battle was the bloodiest of his career but the casualties which resulted were outnumbered by those from a tragic accident en route. Two vessels had arrived late at Great Yarmouth where they found orders to follow on. Leaving the coast however the *Invincible,* with Admiral Totty aboard, struck on Hammond's Knoll, despite the presence of a local pilot aboard, and became a total loss. Totty was saved but Captain Rennie and upwards of 400 men were lost (compared to 256 British seamen lost at Copenhagen). Many of the bodies recovered are buried in Happisburgh churchyard.

Among the first to send letters of congratulation to Nelson after Copenhagen was the mayor of Great Yarmouth, Samuel Barker. In his reply Nelson sent his respects to the corporation and promised: 'If I land at Yarmouth, I shall most assuredly pay my personal respects to you, not only as a gentleman who has shown [me] great civilities, but also as the Chief magistrate of a Borough of which I have the honour to be a Freeman.'[174]

The battle of Copenhagen: engraving by Pickett after J. Clark, from Orme's Graphic History of . . . Nelson, *1806.*

On 16 March 1801, HMS INVINCIBLE
was wrecked off Happisburgh when
on her way to join a fleet with
Admiral Nelson at Copenhagen.
The day following, the Ship sank with
the loss of some four hundred lives.
One hundred and nineteen members
of the Ship's Company lie buried here.

"And the sea gave up the dead
that were in it..."

Revelation 20:13

This memorial stone was given jointly
by the Parochial Church Council and
the Officers and Ship's Company of
HMS Invincible. 1998

This stone in Happisburgh church-yard was placed there by the parish and the crew of the modern HMS Invincible, *to mark the resting place of 119 of the 1801* Invincible *crew, who lost their lives off the Norfolk coast when preparing to sail to Copenhagen with Nelson.*

On 21st May, while he was in the Baltic, Nelson received news of his brother Maurice's death. Maurice had just been promoted in the Navy Office, something which 'has proved the more gratifying to me as there was not any Interest made for it, but devolved upon me as a matter of right'[175] as Maurice had written to his sister Catherine early in April. Ironically he died a few weeks later, on 24th April, shortly before his brother's 'interest' had been about to provide him with a new appointment as a Commissioner of the Customs. Maurice had probably been Nelson's favourite brother and the news 'has naturally affected me a great deal,'[176] as he wrote to Lord St Vincent. 'Six sons are gone out of eight,' he mused. Indeed, 'if I do not get some repose very soon, another will go'. His first thoughts, though were for the widow, and he wrote to his friend and agent, Davison, to ask that 'you will do everything which is right for his poor blind wife . . . I beg you will take the trouble to arrange a proper and ample subsistence, and I will make it up.'[177] His next letter to Davison referred to 'poor Mrs Nelson (for such I shall always call her)', reflecting his own sensibility and his respect for his brother's memory, for 'Mrs Nelson' was in fact Maurice's common law wife, Miss Sarah Ford. A few days later Nelson wrote on the subject again to Davison that

> *if her necessities require it, every farthing which his kindness gave me shall be used, if she wants it . . . for she shall ever be by me considered as his honoured wife.*[178]

Nelson succeeded Parker as commander in the Baltic and remained there until he was relieved in mid June and was able to return home. He left the Baltic on the brig *Kite* on 19th June and arrived at Great Yarmouth on 1st July. Landing at the jetty he was greeted once again by enthusiastic crowds and, expecting him to head straight to the Nelson Hotel (the Wrestlers), the Volunteers assembled on the Market Place. Instead, however, Nelson made straight for the naval hospital to visit, amongst others, wounded sailors from Copenhagen. A young doctor there, Robert Gooch, later recalled the visit in a letter to Sir Walter Scott:

> *I went round the wards with him, and was much interested in observing his demeanour to the sailors; he stopped at every bed, and to every man he had something kind and cheery to say.*[179]

Nelson asked one sailor, 'Well, Jack, what's the matter with you?' 'Lost my arm, your honour' was the reply, to which Nelson, after a wry look at his own empty sleeve, joked, 'Well, Jack, then you and I are spoiled for fishermen'. To each of the nurses he gave a guinea. The hospital, then situated on St Nicholas Road, was built in 1792 by the Navy Sick and Hurt Board. The site is now occupied by Sainsbury's supermarket. It was only a small establishment and was replaced by a new and grander Naval Hospital (the buildings of which still survive) on the South Denes, built between 1809 and 1811. There was time for some refreshment at the Nelson Hotel before Nelson finally left town, his post-chaise and horse decked with ribbons and the postillions dressed as sailors.

Nelson's Great Yarmouth visit was to be the last he would make to his native county. Great Yarmouth's mayor, Samuel Barker, clearly hoped that he might return, however, and wrote to him with that in mind in November, but Nelson was then on sick leave and not in a position to visit, replying:

Faden's map of Yarmouth in 1797 shows the hospital site and the Wrestlers inn.

I have no thought of coming to Yarmouth . . . I never shall forget all your goodness to me, and if ever I am placed in a situation to show my gratitude, I trust I shall not be found wanting.[180]

Perhaps Barker had written following the receipt of a gift from Capt. Hardy. This had been sent to him in acknowledgement of his hospitality to naval officers at Great Yarmouth and comprised a model of an admiral's barge, complete with crew of pigtailed sailors and, seated in the stern with an officer, the figure of Nelson himself.

One unusual memento of his visit remained with Bream, the North Sea pilot who had brought Nelson into port. It was a geranium which had been cleared out of Nelson's cabin in the *Elephant* prior to the battle. Cuttings were given to some of Bream's relatives and one later found its way into Captain Manby's Nelson Museum in the town.

Sir William Hamilton KB FRS, 1730–1803 (engraving by W. T. Fry after C. Grignon). Sir William was ambassador to the kingdom of Naples and Sicily from 1764 until 1800. He died in the arms of Emma and holding the hand of Nelson.

Paradise Merton

NELSON'S OFFICIAL REWARD for the victory at Copenhagen was a viscountcy. He was created Viscount Nelson of the Nile and of Burnham Thorpe on 22nd May and received the news while in the Baltic. The succession, like that of his barony, was to be to his male heirs. Unhappily however his circumstances now made it unlikely that there would be any legitimate male heirs. Nelson was concerned that his titles should not be extinguished on his death and wrote to the Prime Minister to this effect: 'My Dear Sir, I take the liberty of sending you the

manner it is my wish to have the barony of Nelson extended.'[181]
The Prime Minister wrote to the King, who replied that 'The
King is so thoroughly satisfied with the services and ardour of
Viscount Nelson, that he cannot make the smallest objection
to the preservation of the barony in his father's name.' The result was the creation, in August, of a new title, Baron Nelson of
the Nile and of Hilborough, which not only secured the succession in turn to his father, brother William, the sons of sister
Susannah and the sons of sister Catherine, but also celebrated
the parish where his brother held the living and where his father had held it before him.

Between July 1801 and April 1802 Nelson was Commander in Chief of a squadron in the Channel charged with
the defence of the coast. It was not a particularly happy period
and, once peace negotiations began in October, he was able to
take leave for the remainder of the time, and this he was able to
spend at last in a home of his own.

Lady Hamilton had been charged with finding a suitable
property and had chosen Merton Place in Surrey. Purchased
on 18th September, it was occupied by Sir William and Emma
in October, so they were there to greet Nelson when he finally
arrived on 23rd October 1801. The house had some land attached and animals were acquired to graze it, including a
goat brought by Tom Allen. Indeed, Allen's wife became the
dairy maid. In December 1802 Thomas Bolton wrote, 'I have
sent you by Josiah Griggs two cows which I hope you will ap-
prove'.[182] Nelson liked to refer to Merton as 'the Farm' and he
now set about creating there the rural and domestic idyll which
he had always imagined would have been spent with Fanny in
a Norfolk cottage. His separation from Fanny, however, as well

*Emma Hamilton
(engraving by
A. Clement after
G. Romney)*

as the metropolitan tastes of Sir William and Emma, had ruled out Norfolk. Nevertheless, Nelson was determined to incorporate his family into his life at Merton (including, of course, Horatia, whenever this could be tactfully arranged). This was a difficult task initially because they had all, in varying degrees, been shocked by his separation and felt considerable loyalty to the wronged Fanny.

Emma, of course, felt threatened by Fanny, whom she had taken to referring to as 'Tom Tit' (Josiah was 'the cub') and even Nelson, on occasion, adopted this usage. Even before Nelson arrived at Merton, Emma had begun her campaign to divorce Fanny from the rest of the family. Her first allies were, inevitably, the socially ambitious William Nelsons, especially Sarah, to whom she wrote in September:

> You *and your husband are the only people worthy to be by* him beloved. *His poor father is unknowing and taken in by a very wicked, bad artful woman . . . and now he conspires against the saviour of his country and his darling . . . and I am afraid the Boltons are not without their share of guilt in this affair. Jealous of you all they have, with the Matchams, pushed this poor dear old gentleman to act this bad and horrible part, to support a false proud bad woman, artful, and with every bad quality.*[183]

Sarah was happily seduced and soon Emma had taken her daughter Charlotte under her wing. Indeed Charlotte was one of the party in residence when Nelson arrived. Before long her brother Horace (then at school at Eton) was also a regular visitor.

Poor Fanny, the subject of such vituperation, felt keenly the pressure the family were under but the rest of the family were made of sterner stuff. Indeed, in May, Susannah Bolton had written to her:

> *Do not say you will not suffer us to take too much notice of you for fear it should injure us with Lord Nelson. I assure you I have a pride, as well as himself, in doing what is right, and that surely is to be attentive to those who have been so to us and I am sure my brother would despise us if we acted contrary.*[184]

Nelson's father felt the conflict of loyalties most keenly.

Fanny had become like a daughter to him and had been a constant companion. In September she stayed at Wolterton and visited him at Burnham, writing afterwards,

> *My visit to Burnham was one of duty rather than of pleasure I assure you it called forth all my feelings.*

As for a suggestion that he might stay with her in London, 'I told Mrs M. [Catherine Matcham] at Bath, that Lord Nelson would not like you living with me'.[185] His response was:

> *Be assured, I still hold fast my integrity and am ready to join you whenever you have the servants in the London house . . . In respect of this business, the opinion of others must rest with themselves, and not make any alteration with us. I have not offended any man and do rely upon my children's affection that notwithstanding all that may have been said, they will not in my old age forsake me.*[186]

To Nelson he was equally straightforward. Emma, it seems, had been questioning his loyalty to his son, and he wrote in October how he hoped that they might enjoy each other's company

notwithstanding the severe reproaches I feel from an anony-
mous letter for my conduct to you, which is such, it seems, as
will totally separate us. This is unexpected indeed.[187]

Nevertheless,

If Lady Nelson is in a hired house and by herself, gratitude
requires that I should sometimes be with her, if it is likely to
be of any comfort to her.

He finished:

but my dearest son, here is room enough to give you a warm a
joyful and affectionate reception, if you could feel an inclina-
tion to look once more at me in Burnham parsonage.

Any visit to Norfolk was out of the question. Fanny was

*The Nelson Museum
in Yarmouth includes
this model of Nelson in
his study at Merton.*

still a regular visitor to friends and relations there and the possibility of meeting her was something Nelson was not prepared to chance. He was not going to shake his father's attachment to her but offered the hospitality of Merton for a stay, where he, Sir William and Emma would

> be happy, most happy to see you, my dear beloved father, that is your home. My brother and sister [William and Sarah], the dear children [Charlotte and the Bolton twins, Jemima and Catherine] will soon be with us and happy shall we all be, but more so if you will come.[188]

His father was persuaded to accept and, after a fortnight's stay with Fanny in London, went to Merton in November and stayed there ten days before going on to Bath for the winter, where he would see the Matchams.

The Rector's visit to Merton prompted Fanny to make one more attempt at a reconciliation, writing to Nelson, care of his friend Alexander Davison: 'Do my Dear Husband, let us live together. I can never be happy till such an event takes place.'[189] Having been forwarded to Merton the letter was returned to her endorsed 'Opened by mistake by Lord Nelson, but not read'! Clearly there was no hope.

The Rector had also accepted the inevitable and Nelson hoped that he might even be prepared now to take up residence at Merton. In fact rooms were being prepared for him when news arrived from George Matcham at Bath that the Rector was ill. Nelson made feeble excuses for not going to him:

> from your kind letter of yesterday describing my Father's situation I have no hopes that he can recover . . . Had my Father expressed a wish to see me unwell as I am I should have flown

to Bath, but I believe it would be too late; however should it be otherwise and he wishes to see me, no consideration shall detain me a moment.[190]

In fact there was one important consideration which had detained him; Fanny had gone to be with his father. The Rector died the same day that Nelson wrote the letter, 26th April 1802. Two days later he was writing again to Matcham about the funeral arrangements which were to be at Burnham and handled by William:

it is my wish that my Father should be sent attended by a Mourning Coach, Abram [Abraham, his father's servant] *and some other person with him, to be put down at the Parsonage House, from whence he will be buried with all that respect and attention becoming His Excellent Life and the Worthy and Beneficent Pastor of His Parish for 45 years . . . I will in the first place defray the whole of the accounts.*[191]

*Burnham Thorpe
church: photolitho by
Akerman after H. J.
Green, 1885.*

Burnham Thorpe Church. Norfolk.

Other details were considered. He would try to find some new employment for Abraham until when he would pay him an annuity; William was to sort out the details of the service and Matcham should look for the will although he expected nothing controversial in it.

On the question of attending the funeral, however, he hedged:

> *I am not yet fixt whether I shall go to Burnham, my state of health and what my feelings would naturally be might be of serious consequence to myself.*

Fanny, of course, was likely to be there and in the event Nelson did not attend. His father was buried in the chancel at Burnham Thorpe beside his wife.

With the Rector gone there was little to inhibit his sisters and their families from becoming regular visitors at Merton and accepting Emma as a part of their family life. Susannah wrote to Fanny in May to thank her for looking after her father in Bath but felt constrained to say:

> *I am going to Merton in about a fortnight, but my dear Lady N. we cannot meet as I wished for every body is known who visits you. Indeed I do not think I shall be permitted even to go to town. But be assured I always have and shall always be your sincere friend.*[192]

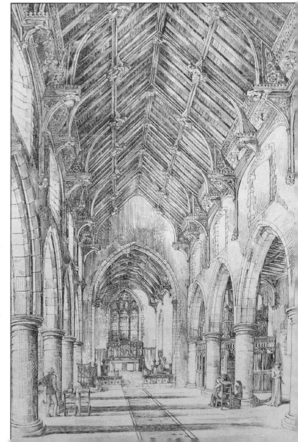

Burnham Thorpe church interior: photo-litho by Akerman after H. J. Green, 1885. The church was extensively restored between 1892 and 1895 following an appeal by the then Prince of Wales.

Gradually, however, this resolution left her. In March 1803 she was seeking Emma's favours in speaking to Nelson on behalf of her nephew William Bolton who had been midshipman on *Agamemnon* and was now a captain. William was also about to be more closely related to the family as he was engaged to his cousin, Susannah's daughter, Catherine. By October 1805 she was writing to Emma that she had seen 'Tom Tit'. It was the same for the Matchams. In January 1803 George Matcham wrote to Nelson that Fanny had

> *called upon us . . . but she did not come in nor make the least inquiry about us, but left a card . . . We should have told her, as we have always declared, it is our maxim if possible to be at peace with all the world.*[192]

By December 1804, however, Mrs Matcham was writing to Emma that

> *My only desire is that we shall not be in the same room* [i.e. she and Fanny] *and circumstances are now so well understood by our friends that I don't think it likely we shall ever meet her.*[194]

OPPOSITE: Letter to William Earle Bulwer, May 1801. Nelson was a prolific letter writer. As his fame grew he would often hear from people claiming a past association with him. In this letter he is happy to recall an old school fellow from the Paston School at North Walsham.

Peace was signed with France in March 1802 and lasted until May 1803, allowing Nelson just one year more of domesticity at Merton, and with his family. A note from Emma to Mrs Matcham in September 1802 sums up the atmosphere at Merton:

> *here we are as happy as Kings . . . We have 3 Boltons, 2 Nelsons & only want 2 or 3 little Matchams to be quite en famille, happy & comfortable, for the greatest of all Joys to our most Excellent Nelson is when he has his sisters or their children with him.*[195]

There was an excursion to the West Midlands and Wales with the Hamiltons in July 1802. At Oxford they were joined by William and family where Nelson, his brother and Sir William all received honorary degrees; Nelson and Sir William as Doctors of Civil Law and William as Doctor of Divinity (Cambridge had already conferred a doctorate of Divinity on William).

Further honours given to Nelson included the conferment of the title of Knight Grand Commander of the Order of St Joachim, a German institution. This had been obtained for him by his former schoolfellow, Levett Hanson, who was then Knight Vice-Chancellor of the Order. It was Nelson's acceptance which prompted Hanson's letter reminiscing about their schooldays.

In June he was able to write to Rev. Stephen Comyn, one of his domestic chaplains who had been his chaplain aboard *Vanguard* at the Nile. He had promised to try to find him a preferment and was now able to congratulate him on his appointment as Rector of Bridgham in Norfolk, a position he held until 1839. Comyn's son, Horatio Nelson Comyn, was later Vicar of Walcott in Norfolk.

On 16th May, Nelson was appointed Commander in Chief in the Mediterranean. Within two days he had embarked on board his ship at Portsmouth and two days later he set sail. One thing he had wished to do, and now had to be hurriedly done, was to see his daughter Horatia christened. Horatia (officially described as his god-daughter with the fictitious surname Thompson) was still with her nurse, Mrs Gibson, at Marylebone. Nelson had made fleeting visits to see her when he could and, indeed, he had been able to have her to stay at Merton for short visits when Sir William was away. He had hoped she might be christened at Merton but instead had to settle for Marylebone where she was baptised Horatia Nelson Thompson on 13th May.

Two occasions, however, Nelson had to miss. The first was the wedding of his niece, Kitty Bolton, to her cousin Captain William Bolton (one of the clergymen's sons who had joined him aboard *Agamemnon* in 1793). Emma hosted the wedding reception at her home in Clarges Street, London. William was shortly to join Nelson's Mediterranean fleet himself. The second occasion was his own investiture as Knight of the Bath which was to have taken place at Westminster Abbey on the following day, 18th May. All had been arranged and his nephews Tom Bolton and Horace Nelson had been chosen as his esquires. Nelson's absence, however, enabled him to provide a handsome wedding present for the Boltons. He chose William Bolton to act as his proxy, and, because anyone acting in this capacity also had to be a knight, Bolton himself was promptly knighted.

While Nelson was at sea, Emma had neither husband nor lover for company for Sir William Hamilton had died on 6th April after a short illness. He died at his house in London in the arms of Emma and holding the hand of Nelson. Nelson encouraged Emma to visit the Boltons at Manor Farm, Cranwich. He wrote from the Mediterranean on 10th June, 'I long to hear of your Norfolk excursion'.[196] Emma did go and found the whole family in residence including Susannah, Eliza, Anne, Tom and Kitty, whose husband had joined the fleet. She enjoyed taking on the role there as arbiter of metropolitan taste and fashion for the Bolton girls, as she had already done for Charlotte (William's daughter). Whilst there, the party attended social events including a concert at Swaffham. Nelson was pleased to hear that Emma had had such a pleasant stay in Norfolk and wrote to her in August, 'I hope one day to carry you there by a nearer tie in law, but not in love and affection, than at present'.[197]

Montpelier House at Swaffham is one of the elegant Georgian town houses around the Market Place from the time when Swaffham was a fashionable social centre. Lady Nelson preferred to live in the town when Nelson was at sea and may have lodged at this house.

Nelson returned to sea without one familiar figure. Tom Allen, his Norfolk servant, was not with him. Allen later apparently told Father Husenbeth, Roman Catholic priest at Costessey, that Nelson had asked him to stay behind to sort out some affairs before joining the ship at Portsmouth and so had arrived there after the ship had left. Family stories even suggest that alcohol might have played a part in his delay. Allen, however, seems to have been a bit of a storyteller because he had actually left the navy some years earlier with £95 of prize money. He returned to Norfolk and was never to see Nelson again. In October 1804, however, Nelson did receive a letter from him asking for a reference. He enclosed Allen's letter in one to Emma, asking, 'Can we assist the poor foolish man with a character'.[198] Allen was still, presumably, looking for employment in the summer of 1805 for Nelson received a letter from Rev. John Glasse, the new rector at Burnham Westgate, asking about him. He replied:

> *Although I kept him many years about me I fear he did not make a grateful return to my kindness to him. He never was my steward nor do I think him able to perform such a service well.*[199]

Perhaps Allen had exaggerated the nature of his duties at Merton, but just how he had disappointed Nelson is not known.

At sea Nelson resumed his practice, when he was able, of corresponding with his relatives, particularly with William and his son Horace (then at Eton) and with Susannah. As always he was keen to help them, financially if possible, though he was always cautious about the state of his finances. He wrote to Susannah in January 1804, remarking,

With respect to Tom [her son], *although I do not know if it
be absolutely in my power to say I will entirely keep him at
College, yet you may be sure of my assistance.*[200]

He expected, though, that he would have more money at his
disposal 'when poor blindy goes the way of all flesh'. This was
Maurice's widow whom he was financially supporting. He was
not willing 'poor blindy' away, however, for he wrote to Emma
in March,

*I could not bear that poor blind Mrs Nelson should be in want
in her old days . . . if you will find out what are her debts, if
they come within my power, I will certainly pay them.*[201]

In April he made a codicil to his will stating that £100 should
be 'annually paid unto the reputed widow of my brother
Maurice Nelson by whatever name she may assume, be it S.
Nelson, S. Field, or any other'.[202] In his letter to Emma he also
confirmed that

*Tom . . . I shall certainly assist at College; and, I am sure,
the Doctor* [William] *expects that I should do the same for
Horace.*

In May 1805 he sent sister Susannah

*a bill for one hundred pounds; and when I get home, I hope
to be able to keep Tom at College without one farthing's expenses to Mr Bolton.*[203]

There was one more family correspondent on his list now.
In October 1803 he wrote to 'Miss Horatia Nelson Thompson
(age 2)', 'My dear Child, Receive this first letter from your most
affectionate Father.'[204] Horatia was very much in his thoughts

now. He had made a second codicil to his will in September 1803 leaving her £4,000 and appointing Emma her sole guardian. In his desire to see her assume his name legitimately he had added that Lady Hamilton would

> *I hope make her a fit wife for my dear nephew Horatio Nelson, who I wish to marry her if he proves worthy.*[205]

Despite the considerable demands of his command in the Mediterranean Horatia's well-being was a continual concern. In his letters to Emma he was keen to hear that Horatia was at Merton with her, although Emma was happier at her town house in London. In his letter in March Nelson wrote,

> *I also beg, as my dear Horatia is to be at Merton, that a strong netting about three feet high may be placed around the Nile* [his name for the Wandle, the stream that ran through the grounds], *that the little thing may not tumble in.*[206]

As usual there were letters from relatives asking favours and so, in April 1804, Nelson was replying to his cousin Rev. Robert Rolfe that he was 'well aware of your obligations to Sir R. Bedingfield' and 'you may be assured that if it is in my power, I will most assuredly promote Mr Bedingfield'.[207] This was Thomas, a relative of Sir Richard and then serving with Nelson. In his reply to the letter from Richard Allott, in May, which had reminded him of Burnham, he reflected sadly that 'Most probably I shall never see dear, dear Burnham again'.[208]

This part of the letter is reproduced on page 11.

Nelson's Mediterranean service entailed months at sea blockading the French fleet in Toulon. When the French managed to escape, Nelson searched the length of the Mediterranean for them before pursuing them across the Atlantic to the

West Indies and back, but without the satisfaction of engaging them. A period of leave was overdue and he returned to England, arriving back at Merton on 21st August 1805.

Nelson was determined to enjoy a family atmosphere at Merton and Emma rallied all the family to join him there. Soon an extra table was needed in the dining room to accommodate all the children, who included Horace and Charlotte Nelson, Tom, Eliza and Anne Bolton, George Matcham junior and, of course, Horatia, who was now in the care of Emma's maid, Fatima.

There was time, also, to use what influence he had in furthering the ambitions of his family. Thomas Bolton was looking for an official position and so Nelson wrote on his behalf to George Rose, Secretary to the Treasury, a long time friend:

> *Mr Thomas Bolton, my brother, is a gentleman in every meaning of the word: his pursuits in life have always been those of a gentleman, first a merchant, now a large farmer; he is a man of business, and probably in either the Customs, Excise, or Navy Office* [would] *carry more abilities than many who have Seats at those Boards. The Customs would please me best.*[209]

Early in September came the inevitable call to rejoin the fleet, and Merton was thrown into the upheaval of preparation. Last minute arrangements had to be made, and farewell visits to old friends.

At Merton Nelson had recreated an idealised version of his family life at Burnham; Merton had been the rectory, a family home full of children; his grounds and animals had reproduced the rectory glebe and the Wandle had been his Burn, the stream that ran through Burnham. After 25 days, however, the idyll ended. On 13th September 1805 he wrote in his private diary, 'At half-past ten drove from dear dear Merton, where I left all which I hold dear in this world'.[210]

The battle of Trafalgar: engraving by Pickett after J. Clark, from Orme's Graphic History of ... Nelson, *1806.*

Trafalgar and its Aftermath

NELSON REJOINED HIS fleet off Cadiz on 28th September. Inside the harbour were the combined French and Spanish fleets. On 19th October he wrote letters to Emma and to Horatia telling them that the enemy fleets were coming out and two days later, on the 21st, he brought them to battle off Cape Trafalgar.

The prospect of battle saw Nelson back in his element. He seemed, it was said, 'quite young again'.[211] The date gave him particular satisfaction. It was, he pointed out, the day of the annual fair at Burnham Thorpe, and he remarked to Hardy that 'the 21st of October was the happiest day in the year among his family'.[212] The reference was, of course, to his uncle's victorious action in the West Indies in 1757. Thoughts of Emma and Horatia were occupying his mind and immediately before the battle he asked captains Blackwood and Hardy to witness one last document in which he left Emma and Horatia in the care of his country, writing also, 'and I desire she [Horatia] will in future use the name of Nelson only'.[213]

At the height of the battle Nelson was cut down by a French marksman. He lived long enough to learn that he had won a great victory. Among his last words to Hardy, as he lay dying, these betrayed his Norfolk roots: 'No, do you anchor Hardy,' he managed. It was an instruction of course, not a question; a confirmation of his determination to remain in command to the very end.

News of Nelson's death reached England on 5th November and the following day Sir Andrew Hammond, Comptroller of the Navy, wrote official letters announcing the news to each

TRAFALGAR AND
ITS AFTERMATH

The Destruction of the Combined Fleet off Cadiz (engraving by N. Spilman, Great Yarmouth, 17th November 1805). This naïve scene, produced in Norfolk, is the first known depiction of the battle of Trafalgar.

'I AM MYSELF
A NORFOLK MAN'

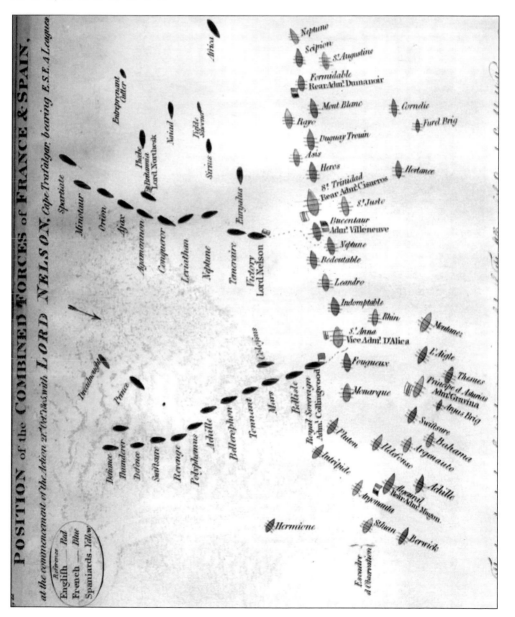

Plan of Nelson's attack at Trafalgar, 21st October 1805 (engraving by J. Godby after W. M. Craig). From Orme's Graphic History of . . . Nelson, 1806.

of the family. Lady Hamilton was at Merton with Mrs Bolton when the letter was delivered and collapsed with a scream. William Nelson heard the news at Canterbury from the mayor, a few hours before receiving the official letter. According to a clergyman who was present, 'the Dr seemed much affected and shed tears, and turned back to his house, applying his white handkerchief to his eyes'.[214]

People across the country were affected by news of Nelson's death but officially the emphasis was on the great victory. In Norfolk there was a round of loyal addresses to the king by the various municipalities, and in Norwich the printer J. Freeman applied to the corporation for permission to produce a mezzotint engraving of Beechey's portrait for sale to the public. (It was published in January.)

Everywhere there were celebrations of victory. On 12th November the mayor of King's Lynn celebrated at the Duke's Head with officers of the army and navy and volunteers. Two days later the First Norfolk Volunteer battalion with the Rifle Corps of the local yeomanry cavalry assembled in the Tuesday Market Place to fire three volleys and on the 21st there was a Grand Ball and Supper at the Town Hall. In Norwich there was a celebratory dinner for the Volunteer Riflemen at the Assembly House on the 13th.

The main celebrations, however, were in December, for the 5th was set as the official Day of Thanksgiving. The day was marked at Great Yarmouth by a ball and supper at the Town Hall. At Thetford the Mayor and Corporation processed to church with the local volunteer corps and in Cromer the volunteer Artillery attended a special service.

In Aylsham there was an elaborate procession to the

church incorporating a band, banners carried by volunteers of
the South Erpingham Cavalry, naval flags carried by sailors accompanying a naval captain on a horse, and a naval lieutenant
carrying a banner inscribed 'the Immortal Nelson'. Afterwards
there were three volleys in the Market Place by the Aylsham
Volunteers, three barrels of beer for the populace and fireworks
in the evening. North Elmham also organised a procession to
church followed by three volleys and a dinner. At Downham
Market the Downham Volunteers attended a service in the
church before processing to the Howdale to fire a *feu de joie* and
then to the various inns for dinner at their officers' expense.

At Norwich the Mayor and Aldermen processed from the
Guildhall to the Cathedral for a service, preceded by companies of volunteers who fired volleys in the Market Place on
their return. Later there was a dinner at Harper's Gardens with
the band of Col. Harvey's regiment playing. Among the decorations in the city was 'a very tasteful illuminated device . . . at
Mr Frewer's window in the Haymarket which bore the motto
'Nelson lives though dead'.[215]

In the village of Whissonsett the 'largest congregation of
people attended at the parish church . . . ever remembered'. Local employers treated the labourers to dinner at their houses,
and plum cake with strong ale was delivered to every poor
family in their own homes that evening.

Swaffham celebrated on 9th December with a Ball and
Supper and on the 14th there was a grand concert of Handel's
Oratorios at the Assembly House in memory of Nelson.

The main county celebration was a Ball at the Assembly
House in Norwich on 17th December, attended by most of the
county's nobility and gentry. The ball was sponsored by the

Norfolk Society and organised for them by local artist Daniel Coppin. The venue was lavishly decorated for the event: a transparent copy of Beechey's portrait by Mrs Coppin adorned the Supper Room and the centrepiece of the Ballroom was another transparency by the same artist featuring Britannia holding a tablet inscribed 'Nelson lives though dead'. Even the dances were themed: 'a hundred couples danced arranged in four sets according to Nelson's four victories'.[216]

Nelson's body finally arrived home on 4th December 1806. In his will, written on 10th May 1803, Nelson had specified that

*In the event that I die in England, I direct my executors . . .
(unless His Majesty shall signify it to be his pleasure that my
body shall be interred elsewhere), to cause my body to be interred in the parish Church of Burnham Thorpe . . . near the
bodies of my deceased father and mother.*[217]

He had confirmed this in his letter to Dean Allott in May 1804:

*I have a satisfaction in thinking that my bones will probably
be laid with my Father's in the Village that gave me birth.*[218]

*Nelson's funeral was
a great public event
and entrance was by
ticket only. Holders
were advised not to
surrender their tickets
to doorkeepers to avoid
the possibility that
they might be resold.*

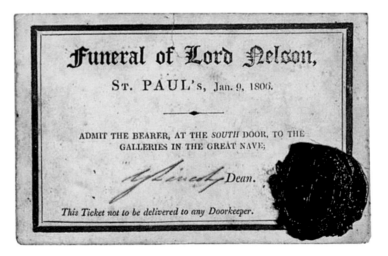

THE FUNERAL PROCESSION of LORD VISCOUNT NELSON, Jan 9th 1806.

PALMAM QUI MERUIT FERAT

NILE

TRAFALGAR

There was no way, however, that the public were going to accept anything but a state funeral and the King concurred. He was to have a hero's funeral at St Paul's Cathedral.

The funeral, on 8th January 1806, was a huge state occasion and public spectacle, attended by members of the royal family and the nobility as well as civic dignitaries and officers of the army and navy, including 31 admirals and 100 captains. Representatives from the family comprised all his closest male relatives, including brother William, brothers-in-law Thomas Bolton and George Matcham, nephews Horatio (Horace) Nelson, Thomas Bolton and George Matcham, and cousins the Rev. Robert Rolfe, Thomas Trench Berney, the Hon. Horatio

The Funeral Procession of Lord Viscount Nelson: engraving by J. Godby after W. M. Craig, from Orme's Graphic History of ... Nelson, 1806

Walpole and the Hon. George Walpole. Custom dictated that neither the female members of the family nor Lady Hamilton were present, a custom that in the circumstances had much to commend it.

Two of the family, in fact, were now among the nobility themselves. On Nelson's death William automatically succeeded to the title of Baron Nelson of the Nile and of Hilborough. The Trafalgar rewards announced in November 1805, however, created two new titles in honour of Nelson's services. On 20th November William Nelson was granted the title Viscount Merton of Trafalgar and of Merton, and was, at the same time, advanced to the title of Earl Nelson of Trafalgar and of Merton. The succession to both was to be to his male heirs or, in default, to the male heirs of his sisters. His advancement to the earldom allowed his son Horace to adopt the title Viscount Merton, later preferring Viscount Trafalgar. There were further rewards to the family. On 28th February an Act of Parliament granted Viscountess Nelson (Fanny) an annuity of £2,000 for life and provided gifts of £10,000 each for Susannah Bolton and Catherine Matcham (later raised to £15,000 each). An annuity of £5,000 was granted to the Earl and his successors in order to support the dignity of the title (only finally abrogated by the Labour government in the 1940s) and a sum of £90,000 was allowed to enable the purchase of a suitable estate to go with the title.

The Earl's new-found wealth and status bore out the weary prediction of Nelson's friend Collingwood (second in command at Trafalgar) who had written:

The first Earl Nelson

I suppose all the public reward of money will go to the parson, who of all the dull stupid fellows you ever saw, perhaps he is the most so. Nothing in him like a gentleman. Nature

*never intended him for anything superior than a village
curate and here has Fortune, in one of her frisks, raise him,
without his body and mind having anything to do with it, to
the highest dignity.*[219]

Collingwood was not alone in his opinion of the new earl. Even
Emma wrote to a friend that William must have 'great courage'
to accept the honour of calling himself by 'that name'.[220] Tact
had never been one of his strong points and now, in his search
for a suitable estate he let it be known that he had his eyes on
Houghton Hall in Norfolk, much to the annoyance of the own-
ers, the Cholmondeleys. As Nelson himself had said, however,
'My brother has a bluntness and a want of fine feeling, which
we are not used to, but he means nothing'.[221] William Repton,
brother of the landscape designer Humphrey, apparently suggested another Norfolk location, Sheringham Park, as an ideal
estate, but it was rejected, having no existing house. Eventually,
in 1814, the Earl bought Standlynch Park in Downton, Wilt-
shire, which was renamed Trafalgar House.

In a last codicil to his will, Nelson had written, on the
morning of Trafalgar:

*I leave Emma Lady Hamilton . . . a Legacy to my King and
Country, that they will give her an ample provision to maintain her rank in life. I also leave to the benefice of my Country
my adopted daughter, Horatia Nelson Thompson.*[222]

His wishes, however, had no legal status and there was no public recognition nor reward for Emma or Horatia though they
were, of course, provided for in Nelson's will. Emma received
£2,000, £400 per annum from the Bronte estate (though the executors felt that this was not part of their concern), and Merton

and its contents (which were valued at £1,430, plus £200 for the hay!).[223] She was also nominated as Horatia's guardian. Horatia received £4,000. There were specific gifts to Nelson's sisters; the sword presented by the City of London to Catherine and the silver cup presented by the Turkey Co. to Susannah. In addition they, and the Earl, each had one third of the residuary estate.[224] Fanny received an annuity of £1,000 for the rest of her natural life.[225] A further £100 was left to be divided among the poor of Burnham Thorpe, Burnham Sutton and Burnham Norton.

The Survivors

EARL NELSON, WHO had achieved more than he might ever have dreamed of, was shattered by the death of his son Horace, Viscount Trafalgar, from typhoid in 1808. Horace was buried in St Paul's, in the same vault as his uncle. After the Countess died in 1828 William, hoping that there was still a chance to get an heir, remarried the following year. The 71-year-old earl's new wife was Hilare, a 26-year-old widow and daughter of an admiral, but there was to be no new heir. William himself died in 1835 and he was buried with his first wife in St Paul's. The earldom passed to Thomas Bolton, the only son of his sister Susannah. The Bronte title, however, did descend in his line, going to his daughter Charlotte who in 1810 had married Samuel Hood. Samuel, later to succeed to the title of Baron Bridport, was grandson of Viscount Hood, Nelson's first commander in the Mediterranean.

Lady Hamilton and Horatia remained welcome within

the extended Nelson family who came to accept without question that Horatia was Nelson's natural daughter. Until 1808 Emma and Horatia made annual visits to the Boltons at Cranwich; indeed in 1806 they were there twice. That summer was particularly convivial with Emma, Horatia and the Earl, the Countess and their daughter Charlotte in attendance. The *Norwich Mercury* reported how Lady Hamilton gave a dinner for the most notable families of Swaffham at the Crown Inn on 25th August. The next day she, Horatia, Mrs Bolton and her daughters, with the Earl, Countess and Lady Charlotte, all went to see *She Stoops to Conquer* at the Swaffham theatre. On

The Market or Butter Cross at Swaffham, with the Assembly Rooms behind.

*Bradenham Hall:
was Nelson's uniform
put out to air on the
bushes here? The
house was home to
the Boltons; was later
owned by the writer
Henry Rider Haggard;
and is now the centre
of well-known gardens
and arboretum.*

the following day Emma, Horatia and the Boltons went off for a few days to visit Rev. William Bolton who was now rector of Brancaster. There were yearly visits to Cranwich until 1808, after which they became less frequent. Their final visit was in 1811. The Boltons had moved from Cranwich to Bradenham Hall, a larger property which they felt more fitting for their son as the heir presumptive to the Earldom. In December Emma and Horatia went up for their housewarming party and to celebrate the wedding of their daughter Eliza to her cousin Henry Girdlestone of Litcham. They were married in West Bradenham church by William Bolton and Emma was guest of honour and chief witness.

Emma may have taken Nelson's uniform with her on this

visit. An old man named Canham, who had once been a page at the Hall, recalled to Rider Haggard how 'Lady Hamilton's wonderful dresses . . . filled the cupboard in the West Room, and how he used to put Nelson's uniform out to air on the lavender bushes in the walled garden.'[226]

Emma never visited Norfolk again and it was the last time she saw Mrs Bolton. Following Nelson's death she had resumed her extravagant social life, but without the means to support it, and descended more and more deeply into debt. Vainly hoping that the government would honour Nelson's last codicil she came to blame the Earl, perhaps unfairly, for her increasing misfortunes, even the Boltons and Matchams feeling that she had some grounds for this. The result was an estrangement between the Earl and his sisters which lasted until Emma's death.

Merton had to be sold in April 1809 and mementoes of Nelson followed, many of them actually Horatia's, but Emma could not live frugally. In 1812 her debts forced a warrant for her arrest. Friends came to her rescue, as they did a second time in 1814, but she then felt compelled to flee to France, taking Horatia with her. They arrived early in July and settled in Calais but Emma was ailing not only financially but also physically and in January the following year she died there. She was buried in the local cemetery.

That same month the British consul in Calais arranged for Horatia to return to England where she was met at Dover by her new guardian, Uncle George Matcham. She lived with the Matchams at their house in Ashfold, Sussex until 1817. George Matcham had always been a restless sort and in 1815 began the practice of making extended trips abroad, taking Horatia and the family with him and renting out Ashfold while they were away. The marriage of his son George junior in February 1817 coincided with a decision to sell Ashfold and spend more time abroad. Happily the wedding marked a reconciliation with the Earl, who had acted as matchmaker in introducing George to Harriet Eyre, daughter of his neighbour at Trafalgar House. He now officiated at the wedding himself and even gave the newly-weds the use of Trafalgar House for a year.

For Horatia, though, it marked another move, this time to Norfolk. It had been decided that she would live with the Boltons. Unhappily Mrs Bolton (Nelson's sister Susannah) had died in July 1813 and Mr Bolton had decided to sell Bradenham Hall and move to Polstead House opposite the church in Burnham Market. Horatia arrived there in February to join her uncle and her cousins Susannah, Anne, and Eliza (Lady Bolton, whose husband was at sea) with her two daughters, Emma Horatia and Mary Ann (another, Ellen Catherine, arrived in July).

Horatia at last was settled and her time at Burnham was probably the happiest period in her life. She soon fell for the local curate, Robert Blake, and although she was still only 16 both her uncles gave their consent, in the summer of 1817, to what was expected to be a long engagement. Early in 1819, however, Blake left Burnham and the engagement was broken off. The new curate was Philip Ward, son of Rev. Marmaduke Ward of Trunch. There were other admirers. Her visit to the theatre at Wells in Spring 1820 inspired a set of verses which were left at her lodgings there. Starting 'Welcome admired Horatia, to our Wells – thou pride of Burnham, and thou Belle of Belles!',[227] they were signed 'Henri', and were possibly by her cousin, Henry Girdlestone.

The reconciliation of the Earl with the rest of the family saw him matchmaking for Thomas Bolton, his heir presumptive, and having already fixed George Matcham up with Harriet Eyre he now engineered Thomas's marriage to her cousin Elizabeth Eyre. Once again the Earl officiated at the wedding, in February 1821.

This happy event for the Boltons was followed by another. Horatia by now had announced her engagement to Philip Ward, the curate at Burnham. Tom Bolton was happy to assist the couple by appointing Ward his honorary chaplain, a post with minimal duties but a modest salary. The pair were married at Burnham by Horatia's uncle, Rev. William Bolton, on 19th February 1822 and the honeymoon was spent at Tom Bolton's home in Sussex. In 1823 Philip Ward was given the living of Stanhoe in Norfolk by Derick Hoste, cousin of Capt. Sir William Hoste, and then in 1825 moved to the living of Bircham Newton. Finally in 1830 he was given the living of Tenterden in Kent by the Earl. Hora-

tia died there in 1881 having brought up nine children (who included a Horatio, a Nelson and a Horatia but no Emma!).

For Fanny, Viscountess Nelson (and Dowager Duchess of Bronte) there was some rapprochement with the family. She recorded that in January 1810

> *The Earl, Countess and Lady C. Nelson came to Bath three weeks since, their good Child not only sought me, but brought her father and mother to my house; I received them, they were much affected, and I think they have received some satisfaction from a shake of my hand.*[228]

When the Matchams (George, Catherine and family) moved to Paris in 1822 they found Lady Nelson there with her son Josiah and his wife and were happy to renew their relationship. One of the girls wrote: 'We see the old Viscountess Nelson

Horatia Nelson is remembered on this stone in the floor of Trunch parish church. Whilst she is not buried here, her husband and father-in-law served as curates in the parish.

almost every day . . . We have drunk tea with her once and are going again this evening.'[229] Earlier Fanny had been the subject of ill informed gossip. On one occasion it was rumoured that 'the Viscountess is going to be married to a Lynn gentleman – one of the merchants there'.[230] It was, of course, not true, and she remained faithful to the memory of her husband until her death in May 1831. The Earl attended her funeral at Littleham in Devon where she was buried close to her son Josiah who had died of pleurisy in Paris a year earlier.

Commemorating Nelson

FOLLOWING NELSON'S DEATH there were proposals for public monuments to him in a number of towns and cities across the country. An attempt to raise a subscription for a national monument failed but there was more success for local campaigns. In Norfolk a public meeting was held at the Shire Hall in Norwich on 30th November. General Money of Norwich, concerned by plans for monuments elsewhere in the country, proposed that 'Surely this county, in which that distinguished hero was born, should be the first and not the last to do the like'.[231] He suggested a pillar of Scottish granite and it was agreed that a countywide subscription should begin at once and a committee be formed to supervise the project.

At a second meeting on 17th December General Money opposed an alternative idea for a monument in the cathedral. Perhaps there might be a case for one in Burnham church, he thought, but he maintained that 'A pillar is the proper attribute

Column at Yarmouth to the Memory of Lord Nelson: drawn, etched and published by J. S. Cotman, Yarmouth, 1817. The top of the monument is shown as originally intended, crowned by a galley (see detail opposite). At the last moment a figure of Britannia was substituted, paid for by Yarmouth Corporation.

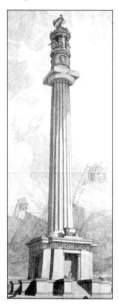

to departed heroes', and suggested a location either on Castle Hill or in the Castle Ditches. Later meetings, however, were deferred as members found themselves unable to agree a suitable site. At one stage a site in Norwich at the junction of the Newmarket and Ipswich roads was favoured. An inability to agree a site seems to have caused the project to fizzle out.

Enthusiasm was regenerated by the signing of the Peace of Paris in 1814 and subscriptions were reopened. Location, however, remained a controversial topic. Norwich Corporation offered a contribution of £200 for a monument on Castle Hill but the committee was now thinking in terms of a coastal location and in January 1815 they decided upon Great Yarmouth. A design still had to be agreed and among those apparently considered was a 130-foot (40-metre) illuminated statue of Nelson by Sir Francis Chantrey, to be placed on a seafront pier. Meeting at Thetford in March 1815, however, the committee agreed designs by the Norfolk born architect William Wilkins. His design was for a pillar similar to one he had already designed in 1808 for Dublin. Instead of the statue of Nelson which capped the Dublin monument, however, that in Yarmouth would have a triumphal galley.

Yarmouth Corporation gave a site for the pillar on the South Denes but the depth of sand there required special foundations which added an extra £2,000 to the original estimate of £7,500. Appeals to Trinity House for financial help, on the basis that the column would serve as a sea mark, met with no success and eventually the design had to be reduced in height by 20 feet (6 metres) in order to match the monies raised. At a late stage the original design for a galley at the top was replaced by a figure of Britannia, a change for which Yarmouth Corporation paid.

The foundation stone was laid on 15th August 1817 at a ceremony attended by the Mayor of Yarmouth and the Lord Mayor of Norwich who proceded to the site from the Town Hall, led by the band of the East Norfolk Militia. The Mayor, Isaac Preston, gave a ball for 350 guests in the Town Hall that evening.

The monument was completed and opened to the public in 1819. In its final form it took the shape of a fluted Doric column of white Mansfield stone, 144 feet (44 metres) high and with an internal staircase of 217 steps leading to a small observation platform at the top. Tragically, the exertion of climbing these brought about the collapse of the Surveyor, Thomas Sutton, who died at the top in June. Above the viewing platform were six Coade stone caryatids carrying a dome upon which stood the Coade stone figure of Britannia. The names of Nelson's four victories, St Vincent, Aboukir, Copenhagen and Trafalgar were inscribed around the capital, and around the pedestal were the names of his flagships, *Captain, Vanguard, Elephant* and *Victory*. In 1896, unfortunately, the Coade stone figures had to be

Gravestone in St Nicholas' churchyard, Yarmouth, recording the death of Thomas Sutton.

replaced by concrete copies which themselves succumbed to the weather and were replaced by replicas in glass reinforced plastic in 1982. Visitors today are surprised to find Britannia facing away from the sea and whilst the reason is not certain it seems likely that she is facing north-west, towards Burnham Thorpe. The Monument was thoroughly restored for the 2005 bicentenary celebrations.

Nelson's Monument in Great Yarmouth is the county monument to the Norfolk Hero but other commemorative memorials are to be found elsewhere in Norfolk.

An early private one stands in the grounds of Curds Hall at Fransham. Built by John Drosiere in 1814 to commemorate the Peace of Paris, it takes the form of an obelisk featuring a small medallion honouring Nelson.

Norwich received its own monument in 1852. A public subscription had been opened in 1847 for a statue of Nelson. Commissioned from the sculptor Thomas Milne, it arrived in Norwich early in 1852 and was put on display in St Andrew's Hall. In 1854 it was erected in the Market Place below the Guildhall. Moved in 1856, it now stands in the Cathedral Close, near to Nelson's old school.

At Burnham Thorpe Nelson was commemorated

COMMEMORATING
NELSON

TOP LEFT: The Yarmouth monument was restored in the 1980s and the figure of Britannia replaced by a fibreglass replica. This head from the figure that was removed is itself from a restoration of the 1860s.

LEFT: The Fransham monument.
BELOW: The statue in Norwich.

in a more practical way with the building of a Memorial Hall in 1891.

Nelson Collections

AFTER HIS DEATH any important relics intimately associated with Nelson gradually came into the hands of national institutions but any item, even remotely connected, was snapped up by smaller institutions and private collectors. Added to these collections were examples of the souvenirs and commemorative items which had fed public demand from the time of his victory at St Vincent and the production of which increased a hundredfold after his death.

An early private collector was Captain George William Manby. Born and brought up in north-west Norfolk, he was the Barrack Master at Great Yarmouth from 1803 until 1844. Keenly ambitious, he saw Nelson, a fellow Norfolk man with whom he claimed a tenuous link, as the model for his aspirations. He was in middle age when Nelson died and felt keenly the difference between their achievements. The best he could do to associate himself with his hero was to pen a song in Nelson's praise which he sang at the Grand Ball in Norwich in December 1805. His dreams of fame and fortune were never adequately realised and when he was forcibly retired from the barracks he consoled himself with his collection of Nelson memorabilia, opening a Nelson

G. W. Manby aged 82: pencil drawing by C. J. W. Winter, Great Yarmouth, 1845. Barrack Master at Great Yarmouth from 1803 to 1842, Manby was now living in a small terrace house in Southtown, part of which was given over to his Nelson Gallery. He died in 1854 and is buried in Hilgay, Norfolk.

Gallery in his little terraced house in Southtown. His catalogue listed only 27 exhibits, of which the most important were paintings by William Joy of the *Agamemnon*, the *Vanguard* and the *Victory*. The gallery proved to have little attraction for the public and after his death in 1854 his collection was left to King's Lynn Museum although some items came into the possession of J. H. Walter.

Also at King's Lynn there is an interesting painting at the Town Hall. It is a copy of a portrait executed by Hoppner for the Prince of Wales in 1801. Lynn Corporation ordered the copy from Samuel Lane early in 1806 and it was delivered in February 1807.

Nelson holdings in the Norwich Museums include the cocked hat worn by Nelson when he sat for Beechey's portrait and presumably that which he then gave to the artist, and a cabin chair made for Nelson in Naples and later used aboard *Victory*. This was given to the museum by Lord Sheffield of Costessey Hall in 1858. Another four were sold in the Costessey Hall sale in 1913. The museum collections also include a plaster bust by Gahagan (for whom Nelson sat in London in 1798), a small collection of letters, family portraits and Nelson scenes, and a pair of pewter plates engraved 'The Nelson Club', made in 1806. The Nelson Club was a patriotic club formed in Norwich in Nelson's honour that year. Some 50 years later it was incorporated into the Norfolk Club. The ensign from the *Généreux* is presently looked after at Roots of Norfolk at Gressenhall and Nelson's St Vincent sword is on show in the Castle keep. The original Beechey portrait still hangs in the Blackfriars Hall.

The Great Yarmouth Museums hold a piece of velvet hanging emblazoned with the legend TRAFALGAR which was

RIGHT: A drape from Nelson's funeral car, now held in Yarmouth Museum. Compare the picture on p. 119.

BELOW: Mr Rivers in action, as depicted in Orme's Graphic History of . . . Nelson, *1806*

The brick is illustrated on page 22. BELOW: Nelson's pencil box.

one of the drapes on Nelson's funeral carriage. It was inherited from the museum in the former Shipwrecked Sailors' Home on the seafront to which it had been given in April 1861 by Captain William Rivers, son of Lieutenant William Rivers who had been one of the naval officers at Nelson's funeral. Lieutenant Rivers had been a midshipman aboard *Victory* at Trafalgar and had lost a leg during the battle, subsequently being admitted to the Greenwich Hospital, where Nelson's funeral carriage was kept after the funeral.

An interesting collection belongs to Paston College at North Walsham. Besides the brick carved with Nelson's initials, there is a pencil box supposedly used by Nelson when a pupil there and once in the ownership of Captain Hardy. A full size copy of the Norwich Beechey portrait hangs in the College library, but is not by Beechey himself nor is it likely to have been owned by Captain

Berry as has been suggested. The collection also includes three Nelson letters; a fourth, the one from Levett Hanson, is deposited in the Norfolk Record Office.

The Nelson collection built by J. H. F. Walter at Drayton Hall was described in 1923 and included a portrait painted from life by a German artist named Schund in 1801, two sauceboats commemorating Copenhagen which were given to Nelson by Lloyds Coffee House in 1801, and a sextant given to Nelson by Captain Suckling. The real treasure of the collection was a sword inscribed, 'Presented by Captain Suckling, commanding H.M.S. Triumph, to Horatio Nelson, midshipman'. Unfortunately the collection is now dispersed and the whereabouts of the sword and other items is not known.

These jugs typify the material produced to commemorate Nelson from his own time to the present day and are from the Ben Burgess collection.

The most significant Nelson collection in Norfolk now was put together by Ben Burgess, founder of the agricultural en-

gineering business which bears his name. His passion for Nelson was fired by his time at the Paston School and his collection began with a biography of Nelson which had been presented to his father as a school prize in 1869. After many years of collecting he vested

The late Ben Burgess developed his interest in Nelson whilst at the Paston School, and his collection of memorabilia forms the basis of the displays at the Norfolk Nelson Museum at Great Yarmouth.

the collection in a charity, the Ben Burgess Nelson Memorabilia Collection, which became the basis of the new Norfolk Nelson Museum in Great Yarmouth. Ben died in 2000, before the opening of the museum in 2002, but he was able to see his long-held dream close to realisation. His collection is strongest on commemorative material in every medium from Nelson's time to the present but there are a number of important original pieces as well. There are letters from Nelson, including one to Rev. Stephen Comyn, a letter to George Matcham from Sir Mordaunt Martin about the Burnham Nile celebrations, letters by Nelson's protégé Capt. Sir William Hoste, and family correspondence to and from his brother-in-law, George Matcham. The picture collection includes an important painting of the death of Nelson by Samuel Drummond, and the comprehensive library includes the original manuscript of Capt. Mahan's *Life of Nelson,* one of the most authoritative of his biographies.

Nelson's Men

AMONG THE NORFOLK men who served with Nelson the closest were the three clergymen's sons who left Norfolk with him to serve aboard *Agamemnon* in 1793, John Weatherhead, William Bolton and William Hoste. Weatherhead was a lieutenant by 1797, when he was killed during the unsuccessful attack on Santa Cruz. Bolton was at the Nile and Naples and was a captain by 1802 when he served as Nelson's proxy at the installation of Knights of the Bath, a service for which he himself was knighted. He married his cousin Kitty, daughter of Nelson's sister, Susannah, in the same year and their first child, born in 1804, was named Emma Horatia after her sponsors. Bolton's later service in the Mediterranean, as captain of the sloop *Childers* (14), was less than satisfactory in Nelson's eyes, and after Trafalgar he left the sea to settle in Burnham Market, although his name remained on the Navy Lists until 1829. In 1821 he took on, with Tom Bolton, the role of trustee for Horatia's affairs. He later moved to Costessey where he died in 1830.

Of the three midshipmen it was Hoste who most closely followed in the footsteps of his mentor and hero. He was at the Paston School some years after Nelson and joined *Agamemnon* in 1793 at the age of 13. After his first action aboard he wrote to his father, 'Captain Nelson is acknowledged one of the first characters in the Service, and is universally beloved by his men and officers'.[232] Hoste was with Nelson at Santa Cruz, prompting the latter to write from his convalescence at Bath to Hoste's father:

> one gallant fellow (Weatherford) is gone. Your dear good son is as gallant; and I hope he will long live to honour Norfolk and England . . . His worth both as a man, and as an officer, exceeds all which the most sincere friend can say of him.[233]

Hoste was one of those entrusted with duplicate dispatches for Naples after the Nile and was befriended by Lady Hamilton there. By the time of Trafalgar Hoste was captain of the *Amphion* (36) but was disappointed to miss the battle, having been sent by Nelson on a mission to Tunis. In March 1811 he was in command of a squadron at the battle of Lissa, where he

Captain Sir William Hoste, 1780–1828. Hoste joined Nelson as a midshipman on board Agamemnon *in 1793. Subsequently he commanded a squadron at the battle of Lissa in 1811 and later commanded the royal yacht,* Royal Sovereign.

*The Hoste Arms at
Burnham Market
bears the name of a
prominent local family
which included one of
Nelson's captains.*

*Captain Berry at the
Nile (detail from the
sketch reproduced on
page 75).*

defeated a superior French squadron, sailing into battle flying
the signal 'Remember Nelson'. Later he commanded the frigate
Bacchante but after a series of distinguished engagements was
forced by ill-health to return to England. He became a baronet
in 1814 and a Knight of the Bath in 1815, marrying Lady Harriet Walpole, daughter of the second Earl of Orford, in 1817.
In 1825 he was appointed to the command of the royal yacht
Royal Sovereign. He died in London in 1828.

Another Norfolk man earned a place as one of Nelson's
'Band of Brothers' (his captains at the Nile). Edward Berry
was born in London but was sent to school at an academy
in Norwich of which his uncle, Rev. Titus Berry, was master.
Lord Mulgrave, a Lord of the Admiralty and former pupil of
the same academy, gained him a place in the navy and he was
promoted to lieutenant after his gallantry in boarding a French
vessel in 1794. He fought under Earl Howe at the Glorious
First of June in 1794 before he was appointed lieutenant on
the *Agamemnon* under Nelson in 1796. He impressed Nelson
straightaway, the latter writing to Admiral Jervis that 'I have,
as far as I have seen, every reason to be satisfied with him,
both as a gentleman and as an officer'.[234] At the Battle of St
Vincent Berry was the first to board the Spanish *San Nicolas*.
After the Nile he was entrusted with dispatches for England
in the *Leander* (50). He was taken prisoner when *Leander* was
captured by the French *Généreux* (80) and was wounded in the
action. Later released on parole, he returned to England where
he was knighted on 12th December 1798. He was in Norwich
in June 1799 when he was a guest at the Mayor's feast but was
back in the Mediterranean by the new year as flag-captain
of Nelson's ship *Foudroyant* (80) and had the satisfaction of

capturing the *Généreux* on 18th February 1800, going aboard her himself to take her surrender. Berry sent the ensign of the *Généreux* to the mayor of Norwich, Robert Harvey, and it was hung above the west window of St Andrew's Hall. It still exists in the Norfolk Museums Service collections.

Six weeks after taking the *Généreux*, and with Nelson no longer aboard, he captured the last French survivor of the Nile, the *Guillaume Tell* (80). Berry earned a reputation as a fighter and when he joined Nelson's fleet as captain of Nelson's old ship *Agamemnon* before Trafalgar the admiral announced gleefully, 'Here comes that damned fool Berry! *Now* we shall have a battle!'[235] On 12th December 1806 he was created a baronet, taking the title Sir Edward Berry of Catton, in honour of his home village. Later he commanded the *Sceptre* (74) and the *Barfleur* (98) before becoming captain of the royal yacht *Royal Sovereign* in 1813. He became a Knight Commander of

Part of the flag of the Généreux. In the care of the Norfolk Museums and Archaeology Service, the full flag is nearly the size of a tennis court. The cost of conservation makes it impossible to put the flag on display.

the Bath in 1819 and a rear-admiral of the Blue in 1821, before his death in 1831.

Of the ordinary seamen it was Tom Allen, of course, to whom Nelson was closest. He had been with him at St Vincent, the Nile and Copenhagen and it is interesting to speculate whether events would have been different if he had been at Trafalgar. Having been looking for employment back in Norfolk he was taken into service by Sir William Bolton at Burnham Market and later moved with him to Costessey. When Sir William died, it was a local doctor, Page Nicholl Scott, whose influence secured him a place at Greenwich Hospital with his wife. When Sir Thomas Hardy became governor in 1834 he appointed Allen to the salaried position of pewterer, a position he held for only a short period before he died later that year at the age of 75.

Many other Norfolk men served in the navy during Nelson's period, some pressed, others volunteers. Many, no doubt, were lost at sea but others are buried in churchyards across the county. Some are recorded but it would make a worthwhile project to identify them all.

On *Victory* alone, there were at Trafalgar, besides Nelson, at least 26 Norfolk men, including seven from Great Yarmouth, six from Norwich, three from King's Lynn, two from Freethorpe and one from Rougham. One of these brings together, in his career, a snapshot of the Nelson story.

When Nelson's Monument was being planned it was decided that it should have someone to look after it and so a cottage was provided on the southern side for a caretaker. The man selected for the job in 1817 was James Sharman. Sharman had been born in Yarmouth in 1785 and at the age of 14 was working at the Wrestlers Inn when he was press-ganged into

Norfolk men on the Victory at the battle of Trafalgar

James Berry, 21, of St John's, Norwich – *killed*

James Browne, 22, of Norwich – *uninjured*

John Bush, 21 – *dangerously wounded*

John Church, 28, of Yarmouth – *uninjured*

John Dixon, 33 – *uninjured*

Robert Farecloth, 22 – *uninjured*

William Flemming, 30, of Yarmouth – *uninjured*

Francis French, 29, of Lynn – *uninjured*

Robert Gibson, 27, of Lynn – *slightly wounded*

James Green, 22, of Attlebridge – *uninjured*

Samuel Jameson, 21, of Lynn – *uninjured*

George Kennedy, 31, of Rougham – *killed*

Thomas King, 32, of Yarmouth – *uninjured*

Thomas Levericks, 20 – *uninjured*

James Mansell, 25 – *killed*

James Melvin, 23, of Norwich – *uninjured*

Horatio Nelson, 47, of Burnham Thorpe – *killed*

Charles Nicholls, 23, of Yarmouth – *uninjured*

Robert Phillips, 21, of Yarmouth – *slightly wounded*

James Secker, 24, of Norwich – *uninjured*

James Sherman, 20, of Yarmouth – *uninjured*

John Starr, 28, of Norwich – *uninjured*

John Thorling, 46, of Yarmouth – *uninjured*

Thomas Tomlinson, 24, of Downham – *uninjured*

William Webster, 21, of Norwich – *uninjured*

John Whitton/Bitton, 23, of Freethorpe – *uninjured*

Thomas Whitton/Bitton, 22, of Freethorpe – *uninjured*

The information in this panel is taken from an extensive database of the crew of Victory at Trafalgar, compiled by Lieutenant Commander Charles Addis RN the navy. He joined the *Victory* after his first ship was wrecked in 1803 and he was aboard at Trafalgar, claiming indeed to have helped carry the wounded Nelson down to the cockpit. He later served aboard other ships but after being discharged from the navy he was admitted to the Greenwich Hospital. He came back to Yarmouth to take up the caretaker's job on the recommendation, supposedly, of Sir Thomas Hardy. In 1856, the vicar of East Dereham, Benjamin Armstrong, visited him at the monument and recorded that 'he seems an honest and seriously disposed old fellow'.[236] Sharman told him that Nelson's daughter, Horatia, once visited him at the column and gave him five shillings and a bottle of wine. A more distinguished

James Sharman (1785–1867) of Yarmouth served aboard Victory *at Trafalgar. His hat on the table beside him carries a* Victory *band. He later became the first custodian of Nelson's monument in the town and the model for Ham Peggotty in* David Copperfield.

visitor was Charles Dickens, who was staying at the nearby Royal Hotel in 1847. The author was apparently fascinated by him and decided that he was ideal as the model for a character in the novel he was then writing. So Sharman became Ham Peggotty in *David Copperfield.*

RIGHT: *John Balls, deputy coxswain of Cromer lifeboat. With two of his sons serving in the Royal Navy, he is one of many Norfolk families whose family tradition recalls an ancestor at Trafalgar – George Brackenbury, sailing master on the* Temeraire.
FAR RIGHT: *John Cannell of Caister lifeboat is another Norfolkman who maintains a close association with the sea and can trace his ancestry back to a Nelson crewman, in his case James Sharman.*

ABOVE: Lord Walpole, current owner of Wolterton Hall where Nelson visited on several occasions, is third cousin four times removed from Nelson.

Notes

1. Palmer, vol. 1, p. 185.

2. Hibbert, p. 257.

3. Harrison, vol. 1, p. 112.

4. Matcham, p. 26.

5. Oman, p. 6.

6. Oman, p. 6.

7. Moorhouse, p. 6.

8. Winter, pp. 40–41.

9. Moorhouse, p. 6.

10. Oman, p. 6.

11. *Naval Chronicle* (1800), vol. 3, p. 195.

12. Matcham, p. 22.

13. Nicolas, vol. VI, p. 18.

14. Pettigrew, vol. II, pp. 262–3.

15. Clarke and M'Arthur, vol. I, p. 9.

16. W. Loads in *The Pastonian* 59.

17. Haggard, p. 449.

18. Manby, *Autobiography* (Norfolk Record Office, Misc. P169A).

19. Fiske, *Notices*, p. 14.

20. Forder, p. 151.

21. *Naval Chronicle* (1805), vol. 14, p. 265.

22. *Naval Chronicle* (1805), vol. 14, p. 89.

23. *Naval Chronicle* (1805), vol. 14, p. 92.

24. Nicolas, vol. I, p. 4.

25. Clarke and M'Arthur, vol. I, p. 22.

26. Clarke and M'Arthur, vol. I, p. 24.

27. Clarke and M'Arthur, vol. I, p. 25.

28. Oman, p. 26.

29. Nicolas, vol. I, p. 44.

30. Nicolas, vol. I, p. 47.

31. Nicolas, vol. I, p. 43.

32. Nicolas, vol. I, p. 47.

33. Nicolas, vol. I, p. 46.

34. Nicolas, vol. I, p. 47.

35. Nicolas, vol. I, pp. 43–4.

36. Nicolas, vol. I, p. 44.

37. Nicolas, vol. I, p. 45.

38. Nicolas, vol. I, pp. 49–50.

39. Nicolas, vol. I, p. 49.

40. Nicolas, vol. I, p. 47.

41. Nicolas, vol. I, p. 47.

42. Nicolas, vol. I, p. 57.

43. Nicolas, vol. I, p. 78.

44. Nicolas, vol. I, p. 88.

45. Nicolas, vol. I, pp. 91–2.

46. Nicolas, vol. I, p. 89.

47. Nicolas, vol. I, p. 91.

48. Nicolas, vol. I, p. 92.

49. Morriss, p. 41.

50. Nicolas, vol. I, p. 98.

51. Nicolas, vol. I, p. 101.

52. Nicolas, vol. I, p. 105–6.

53. Nicolas, vol. I, p. 111.

54. Nicolas, vol. I, p. 126.

55. Nicolas, vol. I, p. 150.

56. Nicolas, vol. I, p. 204.

57. Nicolas, vol. I, p. 145.

58. Nicolas, vol. I, p. 145.

59. Matcham, p. 47.

60. Matcham, p. 55.

61. Matcham, p. 57.

62. Fiske, *Notices*, p. 8.

63. Fiske, *Notices*, p. 26.

64. Matcham, p. 64.

65. Matcham, p. 60.

66. Matcham, p. 61.

67. Oman, p. 104.

68. Matcham, p. 63.

69. Moorhouse, p. 59.

70. Matcham, p. 63.

71. Oman, p. 105.

72. Matcham, p. 64.

73. Matcham, p. 65.

74. Nicolas, vol. I, pp. 281–2.

75. Oman, p. 114.

76. Matcham, p. 76.

77. Nicolas, vol. I, p. 290.

78. Matcham, p. 76.

79. Oman, p. 107.

80. Matcham, p. 72.

81. Matcham, p. 69.

82. Pocock, p. 90.

83. Matcham, p. 68.

84. Matcham, p. 76.

85. Moorhouse, p. 66.

86. Matcham, pp. 87–8.

87. Matcham, p. 90.

88. Nicolas, vol. I, pp. 292–3.

89. Nicolas, vol. I, p. 295.

90. Pocock, p. 95.

91. Naish, p. 72.

92. Matcham, p. 99.

93. Nicolas, vol. I, p. 298.

94. Harrison, vol. I, p. 112.

95. Isaacson, *Nelson's Five Years*, p. 12.

96. Naish, p. 73.

97. Naish, p. 80.

98. Matcham, p. 105.

99. Matcham, p. 100.

100. Matcham, p. 105.

101. Naish, p.95.

102. Nicolas, vol. I, p. 298.

103. Naish, p.223.

104. Matcham, p. 117.

105. Naish, p. 85.

106. Matcham, p. 118.

107. Naish, p. 86.

108. Naish, p. 107.

109. Naish, p. 208.

110. Naish, p. 218.

111. Naish, p. 122.

112. Naish, p. 121.

113. Naish, p. 100.

114. Nicolas, vol. I, p. 356.

115. Nicolas, vol. I, p. 393.

116. Naish, p. 187.

117. Naish, p. 190.

118. Naish, pp. 315–17.

119. Nicolas, vol. II, p. 356.

120. Naish, p. 348.

121. Naish, p. 314.

122. Nicolas, vol. II, p. 357.

123. Nicolas, vol. II, pp. 357–8.

124. Naish, p. 370.

125. Naish, p. 376.

126. Naish, p. 296.

127. Naish, p. 324.

128. Naish, p. 328.

129. Naish, p. 365.

130. Naish, p. 330.

131. Naish, p. 332.

132. Nicolas, vol. II, p. 440.

133. Nicolas, vol. II, p. 451.

134. Matcham, p. 107.

135. Naish, p. 376.
136. Nicolas, vol. II, p. 455.
137. Oman, p. 261.
138. Nicolas, vol. II, p. 453.
139. Nicolas, vol. II, p. 456.
140. Matcham, p. 150.
141. Naish, p. 451.
142. Naish, p. 451.
143. Naish, p. 458.
144. Naish, p. 458.
145. Naish, p. 453.
146. *Norwich Mercury* (13th October 1798).
147. Naish, p. 452.
148. Naish, p. 475.
149. Nicolas, vol. III, p. 138.
150. Parsons, p. 129.
151. Parsons, p. 131.
152. Nicolas, vol. III, p. 322.
153. Nicolas, vol. III, p. 434.
154. Nicolas, vol. III, p. 322.
155. Naish, p. 259.
156. Nicolas, vol. III, p. 412.
157. Naish, p. 531.
158. Naish, p. 540.
159. Nicolas, vol. IV, p. 514.
160. Nicolas, vol. IV, p. 514.
161. Palmer, vol. 1, p. 185.
162. *Norwich Mercury* (15th November 1800).
163. Palmer, vol. 1, p. 185.
164. Oman, p. 416.
165. Naish, p. 580.
166. Naish, p. 580.
167. Nicolas, vol. II, p. 436.
168. Rawson, p. 317.
169. Hibbert, p. 251.
170. Hibbert, p. 252.
171. Palmer, vol. 1, p. 363.
172. Nicolas, vol. IV, p. 292.
173. Nicolas, vol. IV, p. 292.
174. Nicolas, vol. IV, p. 350.
175. Matcham, p. 187.
176. Nicolas, vol. IV, p. 380.
177. Nicolas, vol. IV, p. 378.
178. Nicolas, vol. IV, p. 391.
179. *Lives of the British Physicians.*
180. Nicolas, vol. IV, p.522.
181. Nicolas, vol. IV, p. 423.
182. Naish, p. 600.
183. Naish, pp. 592–3.
184. Naish, p. 587.
185. Naish, p. 594.
186. Naish, p. 595.
187. Naish, p. 594.
188. Naish, p. 596.
189. Naish, p. 596.
190. Matcham, p. 194.
191. Matcham, p. 195.
192. Naish, p. 599.
193. Naish, p. 602.
194. Naish, p. 604.
195. Matcham, p. 204.
196. Gerin, p. 64.
197. *The Letters of Lord Nelson to Lady Hamilton,* p. 135.
198. Nicolas, vol. VI, p. 244.
199. Ron Fiske in *Eastern Daily Press* (7th January 2005).
200. Nicolas, vol. V, p. 363.
201. Nicolas, vol. V, p.441.
202. Nicolas, vol. VII, p. ccxxxviii.
203. Nicolas, vol. VI, p. 429.
204. Rawson, p. 396.
205. Nicolas, vol. VII, p. ccxxxvi.
206. Nicolas, vol. V, p. 440.
207. Nicolas, vol. V, p. 488.
208. Nicolas, vol. VI, p. 18.
209. Nicolas, vol. VII, p. 29.
210. Nicolas, vol. VII, p. 33.

211. Pope, p. 221.
212. Warner, *Nelson's Battles,* p. 188.
213. Nicolas, vol. VII, p. 141.
214. Gerin, p. 106.
215. *Norwich Mercury* (7th December 1805).
216. *Norwich Mercury* (21st December 1805).
217. Nicolas, vol. VII, p. ccxxi.
218. Nicolas, vol. VI, p. 18.
219. Warner, *Trafalgar,* p. 166.
220. Hibbert, p. 389.
221. Pettigrew, vol. I, p. 426.
222. Nicolas, vol. VII, p. ccxl.
223. Nelson's Annuity Book B. Information from Ron Fiske.
224. Nelson's Annuity Book B. Information from Ron Fiske.
225. Nelson's Annuity Book B. Information from Ron Fiske.
226. Lilias Rider Haggard in the *Eastern Daily Press* (17th December 1946).
227. Gerin, p. 238.
228. Naish, p. 617.
229. Matcham, p. 295.
230. Oman, p. 652.
231. *Norwich Mercury* (7th December 1805).
232. Oman, p. 135.
233. Nicholas, vol. II, p. 442.
234. Nicholas, vol. II, p. 175.
235. Pocock, p. 319.
236. Armstrong, p. 45.

A Nelson Chronology

1758   **September 29th,** born at Burnham Thorpe to
        Catherine (née Suckling) and Edmund Nelson.

1767   School at Norwich Grammar School.
        December 26th, death of mother.

1768   School at Paston Grammar School, North Walsham.

1771   **March,** joined *Raisonable* (64) as midshipman under
        uncle Maurice Suckling.
        Voyage to Caribbean on merchant ship.

1772   Midshipman on *Triumph* (74) at Chatham.

1773   **June – October,** voyage to Arctic on *Carcass.*
        Voyage to East Indies on frigate *Seahorse* (38) as
        midshipman.

1776   Sent home ill from Bombay.
        October, joined *Worcester* (64) as acting 4th
        lieutenant. Convoy duty to Mediterranean.

1777   **April 9th,** passed as lieutenant.
        April 10th, joined frigate *Lowestoffe* (32) as 2nd
        Lieutenant. Service in West Indies.

1778   Appointed commander of brig *Badger* (16).

1779   Promoted post-captain commanding frigate
        Hinchinbrooke (28).

1780   Attacked fortress of San Juan in Nicaragua.
        Sent home ill.

1781 **August,** appointed Captain of frigate *Albemarle* (28).
Convoy duty in North Sea.

1782 Service off Canada and in West Indies.

1783 Visit to France, staying in St Omer.

1784 Captain of frigate Boreas (28). Service in West Indies
until 1787.

1787 **March 11th,** married widow Frances (Fanny) Nisbet
in Nevis (WI). Returned to England with her.
Next five years on half pay at Burnham Thorpe.

1793 **January,** appointed Captain of *Agamemnon* (64).

1794 **July 12th,** lost sight of right eye at siege of Calvi, Corsica.

1795 **March,** engagement with French ship *Ca Ira* (80).

1796 **March 1st,** promoted Commodore. Shifted pennant
aboard *Captain* (74).

1797 **February 14th,** Battle of St Vincent.
March 17th, created Knight of the Bath.
March 20th, promoted rear-admiral of the Blue.
July 24th, lost right arm in attack on Santa Cruz
(Tenerife, Canaries).

1798 **March 14th,** hoisted flag on *Vanguard* (74).
August 1st, Battle of the Nile.
November 6th, created Baron Nelson of the Nile and
Burnham Thorpe.
Fell in love with Lady Hamilton.
Involved in Neapolitan politics.

1799 **January 14th,** promoted rear-admiral of the Red.
August 13th, created Duke of Bronte (Sicily).

1800 **February 18th,** captured the *Généreux* (74).
Returned to England with Hamiltons.
November 6th, landed at Gorleston.

1801   **January 30th,** promoted vice-admiral of the Blue.

January 30th (?), daughter Horatia born.

Separated from wife.

March 12th, sailed from Yarmouth to Baltic on *St George* (98).

March 25th, transferred to *Elephant* (74).

April 2nd, Battle of Copenhagen.

May 22nd, created Viscount Nelson of the Nile and Burnham Market.

July 24th, appointed to command squadron in Channel.

August, created Baron Nelson of the Nile and Hilborough.

September 18th, bought Merton Place.

1802   **April 26th,** death of father.

July, tour of West Wales and Midlands.

1803   **April 3rd,** death of Sir William Hamilton.

May 14th, appointed Commander-in-Chief in Mediterranean.

May 18th, hoisted flag in *Victory* (100).

1804   **May – July,** pursuit of French fleet to West Indies and back.

October 21st, Battle of Trafalgar. Death aboard *Victory*.

1806   **January 9th,** state funeral at St Paul's Cathedral.

Bibliography and Sources

Benjamin John Armstrong, *A Norfolk Diary* (London: Harrap, 1949).

Bob Brister, *A Journey Around Nelson's Norfolk* (Norwich: Bob Brister, 1993).

James Stanier Clarke and John M'Arthur, *The Life and Services of Horatio Viscount Nelson* (London, 1840).

R. C. Fiske, *News of Trafalgar and a Lost Portrait* (North Walsham: R. C. Fiske, 1993).

R. C. Fiske, *Notices of Nelson Extracted from Norfolk and Norwich Notes and Queries* (Nelson Society, 1983).

Charles R. Forder, *A History of the Paston School, North Walsham, Norfolk,* 2nd ed. (North Walsham: The Governors, 1975).

Winifred Gerin, *Horatia Nelson* (Oxford: Clarendon Press, 1970).

Henry Rider Haggard, *A Farmer's Year* (Longmans, 1909).

James Harrison, *The Life of . . . Horatio, Lord Viscount Nelson* (London, 1806).

Henry Hibberd, *A History of Burnham Thorpe* (Norwich: Goose, 1937).

Christopher Hibbert, *Nelson: A Personal History* (London: Viking, 1994).

Cecil J. Isaacson, *Admiral Lord Nelson & His Homeland* (Los Angeles: Volt, 1983).

Cecil J. Isaacson, *Nelson's 'Five Years on the Beach' and The Other 'Horatio' Nelson of Burnham Thorpe* (C. J. Isaacson, 1991).

C. B. Jewson, *Jacobin City: A Portrait of Norwich in its Reaction to the French Revolution, 1788–1802* (Glasgow: Blackie, 1975).

Ludovic Kennedy, *Nelson and His Captains*, new rev. ed. (London: Fontana, 1976).

The Letters of Lord Nelson to Lady Hamilton (London, 1814).

Charles Lewis, *Nelson's Monument, Great Yarmouth* (Norwich: Norfolk Museums Service, 1985).

Lives of the British Physicians (1830).

M. Eyre Matcham, *The Nelsons of Burnham Thorpe: A Record of a Norfolk Family Compiled from Unpublished Letters and Notebooks, 1787–1842* (London: Lane, 1911).

E. H. Moorhouse, *Nelson in England: A Domestic Chronicle* (London: Chapman & Hall, 1913).

Roger Morriss, *Nelson: The Life and Letters of a Hero* (London: Collins & Brown, 1996).

George P. B. Naish (ed.), *Nelson's Letters to His Wife and Other Documents, 1785–1831* (London: Routledge & Kegan Paul in conjunction with the Navy Records Society, 1958).

Thomas Nelson, *A Genealogical History of the Nelson Family*, rev. ed. (King's Lynn: Thew, 1908).

Nicholas Harris Nicolas (ed.), *The Dispatches and Letters of Vice Admiral Lord Viscount Nelson*, 7 vols (London, 1845–46; reprinted London: Chatham Publishing, 1997–98).

Carola Oman, *Nelson* (London: Hodder and Stoughton, 1947).

Edward Orme, *Orme's Graphic History of the Life, Exploits,
and Death of Horatio Nelson* (London: Longman,
1806).

Charles John Palmer, *The Perlustration of Great Yarmouth*
(Yarmouth: George Nall, 1872-75).

G. S. Parsons, *Nelsonian Reminiscences: Leaves from Memory's
Log: A Dramatic Eye-witness Account of the War at Sea,
1795–1810 (*London: Gibbings, 1905; reissued London:
Chatham Publishing, 1998).

Thomas Joseph Pettigrew, *Memoirs of the Life of Vice-Admiral
Lord Viscount Nelson* (Boone, 1849).

Tom Pocock, *Horatio Nelson (*London: Pimlico, 1994).

Dudley Pope, *England Expects* (London: Weidenfeld &
Nicholson, 1959).

Geoffrey Rawson (ed.), *Nelson's Letters* (London: Dent, 1960).

John Sugden, *Nelson. *Vol. 1: *A Dream of Glory, 1758–1797*
(London: Jonathan Cape, 2004).

Richard Walker, *The Nelson Portraits: An Iconography of
Horatio, Viscount Nelson, K.B., Vice Admiral of
the White (*Portsmouth: Royal Naval Museum
Publications, 1998).

Oliver Warner, *Nelson's Battles* (London: Batsford, 1965).

Oliver Warner, *Trafalgar* (London: Batsford, 1959).

Colin White (ed.), *The Nelson Companion (*Stroud: Alan
Sutton in association with the Royal Naval Museum,
1995).

Les Winter, *Heritage and Nelson: A Salute to Both* (Les Winter,
1980).

Index

Figures in *italics* denot pages with illustrations